Sometimes, when we fear the
world that surrounds us, only
help us make sense of everyth

AWAKENING THE
SLUMBERING
DRAGON

DAVID SHAW

CONTENTS

DEEP TRANCE MEDIUMSHIP

Deep trance mediumship is achieved when a spirit medium enters an altered state of consciousness that allows spirit energy to utilise the medium's physical capabilities. The spirit energy may then be able to communicate verbally with an audience in the physical world, thus bringing forward accurate and informative information that may enhance the bridge between the two dimensions.

This six-year experiment involved many mediums from our world that were able to blend with those from the spirit dimension, with a view to bringing forth knowledge of our complex existence.

The spirit energies that came forward in this experiment are amongst the most knowledgeable souls in our Universe. They also dwell in a timeless environment, which gives them the natural ability to peer into our physical future. During 2023, the spirit energies asked us to make the information brought forward from these monthly trance sessions available to the public so that we could prepare ourselves for whatever was about to commence in our world.

Deep trance mediumship should only ever be attempted in the company of a highly trained and experienced tutor. Do not try this at home!

INTRODUCTION

by David Shaw (Trance Co-ordinator)

In the year 2011 I decided to write a book about my life as a psychic medium. In general, the book was well received and as a result I was offered a publishing contract two years later. The publisher was happy to use my original manuscript with only a few alterations, but I was asked to add in a small chapter at the end. Their reason being that the book was now two years old, and as it was an autobiographical account of my entire life then it was only fitting that the book reflected my complete timeline and was of course up to date.

I suppose I expected this final chapter (epilogue) to be in sync with the rest of the somewhat light-hearted account of my life up to that point, but instead I was given a rather disturbing premonition of what my life in the future would be like – and the world that encompassed it.

My book 'An Average Joe's Search for the Meaning of Life' describes what it's like for an 'Average Joe' like me to frequently receive messages and information from a source that's not only invisible to the human eye but remains entirely unknown in any quantity to most of this huge planet's population.

For the most part, life in general exists in my world just as simply as it does in yours. However, when something occurs in our world that drastically changes the way in which we behave or function then this event will affect you just as much as it does me. The only difference being that I will often receive prior knowledge of whatever comes around every corner, even though I now sit at my keyboard more than ten years later after receiving that initial forecast - and only now will I be furnished with the capability to finally find out just what all the fuss is about.

The final chapter in my first book referred to a great challenge that humans would soon face – where our very existence would come under threat. The only clue that I ever received was that there would be massive civil unrest in our cities that would take many years to resolve. The cause of this was never revealed to me at that time.

As a trance medium, I receive information direct from spirit guides. These guides exist in a world that is devoid of 'time', which allows them to view events in our world in a timeless fashion. Imagine watching a recording of a television programme with the ability to fast forward to any part of the recording and witness any event, rather than have to watch the entire programme stage by stage, minute by minute – or in this case year by year. I suppose, in a way, it's like watching a movie on television, and a friend who has previously watched the movie at the cinema then decides to spoil the ending for you.

As I previously mentioned, it was more than ten years ago that I was advised by my spirit guides that our world would endure a global event that would radically alter the lives of everyone on it, and every year since I have been sitting on tenterhooks, nervously waiting on this event occurring, yet thankfully it has still to surface. At times, I wondered if I had picked up the information wrongly. Yet, I knew that these guides were working closely with me during the writing of the epilogue – and they certainly wouldn't have been wrong in this forecast as I have never known them to make wrong predictions. As I stated before, they have the ability to witness events in their capacity so it clearly isn't predictions in their part – more like eyewitness accounts. So, the fear has remained within me to this present day, but the uncertainty is now beginning to dwindle as I can feel a decisive change in the energies all around me. It's not so much 'will' this happen- more like 'when'.

In the year 2017 I was asked by a local spiritual organisation if I would coordinate and train a trance mediumship group. This would entail teaching mediums how to work in a trance-like state in order to invoke suitable conditions for working with higher dimensional spirit guides - the main objective being to receive information and guidance directly from spirit people by channelling their voices through the mediums. In other words, spirits would talk through the mediums whilst they were in a state of sub consciousness.

In January 2019 during a meeting of this local trance group, one of my trance guides spoke through me whilst I was in a deep state of sub consciousness. The group then witnessed my guide stating that our world would never quite be the same from that moment onwards. When I was later informed of what was said I instantly knew that the time had finally arrived. At that point in 2019 the Coronavirus pandemic was still very much in its infancy and most of us firmly believed that it would be contained in China, where the outbreak started.

On further research during the following few months, we discovered through our trance group that the Coronavirus epidemic would become worldwide and cause great suffering to millions of people. However, we were also informed that the virus was only ever the catalyst for the real troubles that were still to come. In essence, the financial difficulties left behind by fighting the virus would be the main reason for major civil unrest.

'The Stars from Above Sanctuary' is based in Prestwick, Ayrshire – about thirty miles south of Glasgow. The group is run by three friends who have spent a lifetime working with the spirit world in many different facets. When the three ladies asked me to start a trance mediumship training group in 2017, I was a bit reluctant at first, due to the fact that these groups rarely last any longer than a few weeks. This is due to the fact that it can be extremely challenging for students to be able to channel spirit people and inevitably they prefer to move on to other spiritual endeavours. However, this time a lot of the students were complete novices with little mediumship training – but with a great willingness to learn from the beginning.

Naturally, I had reservations about just how far this could go, yet amazingly it seemed to work extremely well and over the years the group grew from strength to strength, not only in numbers, but in their natural ability to instigate fantastic connections with the trance guides – and bring forward incredibly accurate information through spirit channelling.

In January of this year (2023) I was informed that I would no longer be training the trance group. The trance guides would now take over and I would just be tasked with receiving their instructions and passing this on to the group. I was further informed that they had chosen four members of the group to work in a deep trance mode to bring forward important information through channelling. The rest of the group would act as witnesses and also assist with the necessary energy required to keep the trance sessions functional. For the purposes of this publication, the four trance mediums are referred to as 'vessels' and the rest of the group are referred to as 'sitters'. As it was myself co-ordinating the process, I am referred to as simply - the co-ordinator.

I was advised that they had chosen the four specific trance guides as they were the best placed mediums to be able to handle the information being brought forward. Furthermore, they regarded the sitters to be just as important as the vessels in this process – insisting that the team assembled had taken six years to blend together. Finally, I was informed that I was not chosen as one of the four main trance mediums. The reason for this shall remain private to me. However, I was asked if I would act in reserve if required and was subsequently used on the months of July and December. A stand-in co-ordinator was used whilst I was the designated trance medium.

The following trance-mediumship transcripts were taken as they happened throughout the year 2023. The identities of those involved were withheld at the group's request. The four trance mediums asked that we only identify them by their first initial – **K**, **M**, **J**, and **A**. A fifth trance medium was also used on the month of October and that medium's initial is **S**. My own initial **D** was used for my trance sessions previously stated.

The spirit people that came forward with information chose an identity to help facilitate with this publication, although they stated that they don't use names to identify themselves in their habitual dimension.

I personally like to think of the trance guides as just fragments of a huge data hub, orbiting somewhere offshore - perhaps millions of light years away, yet seemingly only a whisper away from our very thoughts. I often visualise the huge data hub as an **I**nformation **S**haring & **A**nalysis **C**entre, where all life is experienced before being mutually evaluated.

Before each of the monthly trance sessions in 2023, the whole group took part in specialised trance meditations that were conducted by myself and the spirit guides who work with me. Those meditations gave an insight into what information was going to be brought forward during the trance sessions. This allowed the sitters to prepare questions for the sprit people to answer. After each of the monthly meetings had ended, the information was then summarised with a view to highlighting any significant points of interest and whether any forecasts came to fruition. This was a joint task between myself and the guides, making sure that my own opinions would not influence or interfere with the information received.

It is worth noting that readers of my other books may be forgiven for thinking that all the information being brought forward in regard to the forthcoming major conflict in our world has already been spoken about in great detail. However, this experiment involved several different mediums all with their own specific spirit teams to guide them. It became clear very quickly that everyone was speaking from the same hymn book. The inevitable had suddenly become… the inevitable.

The final trance session before this experiment began was held on the 12[th of] January 2023. A trance guide, channelling through myself, informed the group that the forthcoming events would be **the most challenging times ever faced in the entire history of our planet.**

Please, I beg of you, take a few moments to let those words sink in before proceeding.

FEBRUARY 2023

*The following transcripts were obtained on Thursday 16th February at The Stars from Above Sanctuary, Prestwick, Ayrshire, Scotland. Ten sitters, one co-ordinator, two trance mediums (**K & M**) and two trance guides (**The Blossom & Oephilia**) were involved in this session. The Blossom was the first vessel to come forward.*

Co-ordinator (C): "Thank you for coming forward."

The Blossom (K): "It is an honour to be here."

C: "Is the energy suitable for communication?"

V: "Yes, I will speak, but my chosen words may be few, and then another may step forward. I wish to address the question of protection. I wish to speak of protection of the circle. We are here to protect you. You are surrounded by warrior angels, by the horses, and they will circle you for protection. They are always around you, so that if I step out of the circle then they are always here. It is just that I am using the mouthpiece at the moment but I will not leave the room. I shall not let them pass - those who we do not wish to speak with you shall never pass through. You are forever protected. You have the shield of protection and we honour and respect you. We are happy that you are here and you honour us by being here."

C: "Thank you for those comforting words, they are much appreciated. Will we have the opportunity to ask some questions?"

V: "Of Course."

C: "Or do you wish to give us some information before the questions?"

V: "Please proceed with questions."

3

C: "Thank you. Who would like to ask the first question?"

Sitter 1 (S) "Good evening. My question is about the forthcoming spiritual awakening that we are all about to experience. In my meditative state, I have been witnessing tsunamis and earthquakes on our Earth but the most beautiful thing for me is that my mother has been gone for 52 years and yet she still comes to me and instils hope within me. So I wanted to ask what's going to happen to this group, are we still going to move forward?"

V: "As regards to the big awakening, there are of course those who slumber on your planet, but we are working very closely with the Earth - and those in this group who have become awake, and that is very, very special. You are able to communicate with spirit – either through your mind or through your thoughts, or maybe through some other form of written communication, and that is part of your awakening, but what we require from you now is that you help others to see this awakening. For each of you here are tied to this Earth and we have a great affinity with the Earth. We are forever nurturing you, each of you is like a little cell within the Earth and that cell magnifies with other little cells in the group and you come together for a function. That function is to facilitate the awakening of the Earth – and of the human beings of the Earth.

"The Earth is a being of its own with its own energy and each of you collates the cells together to create a function for the Earth and for the spirit – for we are tied together and we work closely. The work that we achieve in the spirit world is not possible without the work here on the Earth plane, where you must come here because your body belongs to this Earth, but your spirit and your soul belong to the spiritual realms. And you are working here and your little cells gather to create this circle and many other circles and each of you will awaken one and other – just a little drop at a time – we have to dilute the energy because it is a force of reckoning and many may be taken aback by the energy's power but each of you has just a little work to do and you will awaken yourself as you become more aware and make others aware – drip-feeding just a little at a time – very slowly."

"Does that answer your question?"

S: "Yes it does, thank you."

V: "You are most welcome; I give you my respect and my honour."

C: "Anyone else have a question to ask?"

Sitter 2 (S): "Good evening. We are very much aware of Mother Earth accelerating her energy and this is why all the traumas are soon to be happening. I just wanted to ask if there is anything that the trance mediums and sitters in this group can do to make the energy stronger and help others to awaken."

V: "Thank you for your question. The circle is complete and each of you has the same importance in the circle. Some of you may have a mouthpiece but each of you has an equal energy and without your energy we could not speak. We need you – we need you all, and all that we ask of you is that you relax, that you experience this experiment – for it is an experiment, and that you take your place in the circle."

"We also ask that whatever is said here is contained here and do not invite speculation from others. What is said can be discussed with each other so that your energies can gel and harmonise together for that is the way the circle will work. Harmony and respect, does that help?"

S2: "Yes it does, thank you."

V: "You are welcome; I give you my honour and respect."

C: "Sprit friend, I have been informed that there will be a trigger event on the 7th of March. Will this be a significant trigger for us to watch out for, or will it be a subtle event that will become more apparent as the linear days and weeks progress?" "Also, is there anything particular we should be looking out for on the 7th of March?"

V: "You should contain yourself. Those who play with fire will be burned. But like a candle within the candleholder, you can contain your little flame and watch those around you burn. That is not anticipation of a major catastrophe but it is merely to say that if you contain yourself then you can witness the chaos of those around, because we must give back to the spirit. The energies given to the Earth are borrowed – we borrow from the Earth and the Earth borrows from us – and sometimes it has to be taken back. The energy has to go back to the spirit world and sometimes it can jar with the energies and with the Earth, but the Earth needs this. It is imperative to sustain this as we must contain the balance."

"Does this answer your question?"

C: "It does, very much so. So, the energy that we return to the spirit world, would this be the small butterfly which has left and has still to return?"

V: "Yes, there are many who must return to the spirit world but they know this is their way and this is their path. The equilibrium must return to the Earth as it is presently out of sync."

C: "Thank you, can I ask one more question please?"

V: "Yes of course."

C: "How many other trance groups like this are functioning at this precise moment in time?"

V: "We have a formula and we must have everyone working in a certain way. There are many, many groups (some groups only have 3 people and some have many). If you can contain your group then you may find that it can overlap with other groups and this is the way that we need to work. Each group has a focus, has a function, and must all work the same - for they must awaken others too. There are many who slumber, and their slumber has gone on for too long."

C: "Thank you. Does anyone else wish to ask anything?"

Sitter 3 (S3): "Can I ask please – the words spoken here that are going to be in a book, are the other groups going to also write a book?"

V: "That will be their decision but these words will come out and the word will be spread round, and others may have the inspiration to do this also. We don't mind."

C: "For the purposes of the book, how will we identify the energy that now communicates with us?"

V: "My medium has referred to this energy as 'The Blossom' but we do not deal with names although we are happy in this instance to have a name if that pleases you. We are not just the one energy but we are many and just like we do not like you to name Gods, we know that people on the Earth plane must choose a name, but we are happy for you to choose a label for identification just so that you may communicate within your written word."

C: "Thank you, that is most appreciated. It has been an absolute pleasure to begin our journey this evening and we ask that you continue to work with us for the rest of the evening and with the medium who works with you. We will endeavour to print these words exactly as said and we will not express any opinion whatsoever. We will just print what has been said and let others decide on their fate, if that is okay with you?"

V: "We are happy for you to discuss the words, sometimes we may be a little bit cryptic and you may wish to decipher this. I just want to end this session here to say that the energies around you are very, very strong and we will attempt to dilute them a little."

"In future when sitting in the circle you may feel physical energies around you and you may experience communication from other means that you will have to decipher for your written publication."

"I bid you good evening and I honour you and respect you."

C: "We honour and respect you as always. Thank you very much for coming forward."

Co-ordinator (C): "Welcome friend."

Oephilia (M): "Thank you. Welcome to you all. Can I just start by saying that every individual in this room is as important as the next – and you are a team. You are part of a physical team, whereas we are a spiritual team. There are many of us and we are all keen to speak – and we will speak. Is there anything you would like to ask?"

C: "I think there are some questions we would like to ask."

Sitter 4 (S4): "Can I ask a question please?"

V: "Most certainly."

S4: "Every day when I'm sending planetary healing, I have been noticing that the way I have to send the healing is different. I have to concentrate on what I would see as lay lines or cracks in the Earth. Could you help me with this and see if it's maybe something that we all could do as an intention for planetary healing?"

V: "Your planet is in great stress at the moment and therefore the significant areas of stress are the first that are going to be impacted upon so that is why you are very much connected - you are actually in tune with the team that is working in these ways. The lay lines, the stress on the planet, on the physical planet, has been enormous – not just on the lay lines but on the flood plains, and the damage that has been done has been happening for many, many years. It is known that the powers that be know what they are doing but greed sustains all for them, however it cannot and it will not continue as it is not sustainable. That is why we need everyone to start coming together and realising the reality of what is actually needed to live happily and peacefully on this planet."

"This is not going to happen overnight but we are well on the road to starting it. Things are changing and anything that you can send out – healing thoughts being sent out there where it is needed – sending the light out and sending the rays out – and everywhere that light goes out in turn brightens a dark corner. We have to get in to all these dark corners and we need to spread the light."

"Does that answer your question?"

S4: "Yes thank you."

V: "Thank you for asking."

C: "Any other questions?"

Sitter 5 (S5): "Can I ask a question please?"

C: "Yes you may ask."

S5: "Thank you. Good evening. The question I would like to ask is are there Governments aware of all that is going on and can we influence them or can you influence them to do things to help this world?"

V: "We are well in front; I can assure you. My medium has a huge interest in some of the conflict areas within the physical planet because she needs to be aware – because we communicate with her. A prime example of what you are talking about is yes, the Governments know – there is much corruption in the Governments, but we have placed essential people who have contracted to come to the Earth to undertake what is happening during this very, very difficult period within this planet."

"A prime example of this is Zelensky, the leader of Ukraine. He didn't just appear from nowhere. He made a contract and he is a highly spiritual soul that has come down, and there are many others who are placed all over this physical world and they are starting to spread the light. You only have to look at the difference that the presence of one human being – and the spirit of that human being connecting with the soul and contracting it to come back and be there when needed. In a sense you have all contracted to be here in this event that is happening – this quest – The Awakening, or whatever title you wish to give to it."

"So yes the Governments are corrupt. Power is beautiful – but power can be corrupted. Yet we have power and you have power – it is what you do with power. Fear not, fear is the thing you have to be aware of. Do not be afraid and do not let fear enter your spirit as your soul doesn't accept fear, it is the spirit that is here on the journey, on the physical plane, it is the little traveller that brings all the knowledge back to the soul."

"I don't know if that has answered your question?"

S5: "It does and thank you very much."

V: "This group hasn't happened overnight, it has been in planning for a long, long time as are all the other areas that we are trying to influence to move things forward."

C: "Spirit friend I was previously informed in the last publication that 'The End of the Beginning' or 'the light at the end of the tunnel' so to speak, will be many linear years from now. Are you able at this precise time to elaborate on this any further?"

V: "It is difficult because individual choice comes into play. We can see that there is potential for things to turn around and be much more positive, but equally there has to be free choice – and this is what it is all about. Where are we all going to stand? Where are you going to stand when it all happens? And we all know things are going to happen – fear not as fear is the problem. Once you let fear come into your auric field then all sense goes out the window. Be true to your trust; be true to your faith; be true to your light and be true to the contract that you signed before you came."

"We will not give you anything specific because it creates anxieties and expectations, but I will say to you that there are going to be a number of events in different parts of the world that are going to come together, and for those areas there will be impacts. This has happened before and it will happen again, and one of the things we say is that although it's very hard for the people that are here, with yourselves and your loved-one's, things will happen and the balance has to be reset. It will be reset but it depends on human interactions with each other and that will determine how long this process takes."

"Does that answer your question?"

C: "Yes it does, and I know you can't elaborate in great detail but it does confirm what many of us have been getting through from our guides."

C: "Anybody else wish to ask a question?"

Sitter 6 (S6): "Can I ask a question?"

C: "Yes of course."

S6: "I was just listening to you there and it was about, you know, things are going to happen and basically we are not going to be able to stop it. I'm working in an environment where I'm seeing an awful lot of poverty and malnourished children and for a worker who has worked in this field for a very long time it is very difficult to watch. But what I'm hearing from you is that this is their life choice and before they came into being then that was what their contract was, and they are not able to change it."

V: "As a human you can always interact and create a change, perhaps in a circumstance that can help an individual who is in the shadows of darkness through no fault of their own. So, there is always hope as hope is what sustains us and makes you get yourself up and dust yourself down. Remember we have been on many planes and we have experienced what people will be experiencing on this planet every day so it's a reflection of where things have gone wrong. But do not despair because for every action that improves one individual's life then that light shines. The people that are here who are inevitably going to pass back to spirit very soon – that is part of their contract and I can assure you that because they know that they are coming home they will be most welcome. It is the ones that are left behind on the physical plane that still do not have a full understanding and will have the biggest issues."

"I don't know if that helps in any way?"

S6: "Yes it does, I do have a lot of hope."

V: "I think I would say fear not as fear changes nothing.

C: "Friend, can I ask a question please? We know that there are great challenges ahead, perhaps the greatest challenges we have ever experienced, and yet our population has never been bigger. There have never been more spirit energies returning here of their own free choice, even though what they are about to experience once they arrive here is going to be incredible. Are these energies returning because they know what is coming and they now have a chance to redress issues that they had in previous existences with conflict on this planet?"

V: "They return because they are at a stage in their development where that spirit is required to revisit, and in essence that is how the soul develops. The spirits have to go out there and experience everything and bring it back to the soul as the soul is the knowledge base. The soul is like a huge library base and contains any experience that one can ever have."

"So, they are coming back with the sole purpose of hopefully creating situations that will awaken us."

"Does that answer your question?"

C: "Yes thank you. So, every soul is different and has their own individual plan?"

V: "The spirit is the bit that is in your physical – it comes with you. It is our little soldier that we send out. The physical body is nothing. I would say to you to think about that little spirit in your physical body on this physical concrete plane – it is not the easiest of existence. Talk to it; engage with it; develop your relationship with it, as it is that spirit that will come back to the soul, to the essence. The soul is part of the essence, it's the facet of the essence and it is that knowledge that we need. Just as you want questions from us – we need questions from you. We need people to bring back information about what is happening – not just from this plane, but from many planes."

C: "Thanks you for coming forward friend, it is much appreciated. We will now let you rest as we bring back the medium."

V: "Thank you. Love and light to you all."

C: "And to you, many thanks."

Summary – February 2023

The first of our trance meetings brought a plethora of information through from spirit guides 'The Blossom' and 'Oephilia'.

The Blossom began by confirming to us that we would be protected at all times during the trance sessions. This is vital during this kind of work and it is most important that whoever runs a trance group is aware of all energies present within the room and would know instantly if any of the group was under any kind of threat.

I asked The Blossom if there would be a significant event happening on the 7th of March as I had foreseen this date in a meditation that signified unrest in the streets of Great Britain. The answer given invariably put me back in my box, so to speak, and understandably refrained from any specifics. This would be a distinct pattern over the coming months, where the guides would paint a picture of a glass half full, rather than half empty. The reason being that any major unrest on our planet would be looked on differently from the eyes of the spirit dimension, where life is eternal and death has no function or relativity. Indeed, any major conflict on our planet would be seen as opening up endless opportunities to experience the highs and lows of physical life.

There was no major unrest on the streets of Great Britain on the 7th of March. However, on that date the UK Prime Minister made a statement that his government would now take back control of our borders once and for all. Furthermore, this would involve refusing small boats of immigrants from arriving on our shores from Europe.

In many ways, this change of policy from the UK Government could be a significant factor if conflict arose overseas. Understandably, there were large scale protests in response to this statement, not only in the media but also on the streets of London.

Oephilia confirmed that things are going to happen and that life will soon be much more challenging for everyone on our planet. Oephilia stated that the guides need information back from us, even though they are aware of our upcoming future and the events that will take place. This suggests that being here right now and about to experience whatever comes our way is not only a great challenge but also a unique opportunity to experience life in the front line, before returning home to share this personal knowledge with all who wish to listen to us.

Perhaps this Great Awakening that we have been promised really will save us from ourselves. It may depend on whether we wish to view the glass as half full.

Oephilia also mentioned people being on Earth as part of their contract. This would become a regular statement over the sessions and hinted that we are here on a specific agreement previously signed and honoured.

MARCH 2023

*The following transcripts were obtained on Monday 20ᵗʰ March at The Stars from Above Sanctuary, Prestwick, Ayrshire, Scotland. Nine sitters, one co-ordinator, two trance mediums (**J & A**) and one trance guide (**ISAC & CHRIS**) were involved in this session. ISAC was the only guide to channel information as CHRIS was suddenly needed to aid a recently deceased gentleman with the passing to spirit.*

Co-ordinator (C): "Thank you for coming forward."

ISAC (J): "You're welcome."

C: "How is the energy for you this evening?"

V: "Excellent."

C: "Good. Friend, we know that you do not use identities as we do for communication. So, for the purpose of the publication, do you wish to furnish us with an identity that we can relate to, or may we pick an identity of our choice?

V: "You may choose one."

C: "Is the name ISAC suitable for you?"

V: "That is fine with us."

C: "Thank you. May we ask some questions?"

V: "Yes."

C: "We spoke earlier with the medium that you communicate through, in regard to the upcoming events in our physical world that we will inevitably find disturbing. Can you give us some comforting words that we can successfully get through this and come out the other side better spiritual beings?

V: "The simplest solution is to keep yourselves grounded and clear of all negative thoughts."

C: "Thank you. Do you have any timeframe as to when these events will be at their worst?"

V: "Time is irrelevant."

C: "We understand, thank you."

Sitter 1 (S): "Can I ask a question?"

C: "You certainly can."

S: "Do you have any advice for the medium you work with as far as developing?"

V: "You have to be able to trust yourself and look forward, rather than back the way.

C: "Thank you friend."

C: "Can I ask you about the medium who earlier went into a trance state, bringing forward a spirit person who appeared confused. Does this spirit need assistance from us or from yourself?"

V: "It was just a spirit passing over and checking in. Someone needs to ground themselves before trance."

C: "Do you mean the trance mediums need to ground themselves before deep trance?"

V: "Yes."

C: "Thank you. Pleased to assist the spirit person with the passing over to spirit."

Sitter 2 (S2): "Due to the pandemic, the Health Service suffered and appears to be still under extreme pressure. Is this the Governments way of privatising the Health Service?"

V: "It is what it is. We cannot interfere."

Sitter 3 (S3): "Everybody at the moment appears to be surrounded by fear - presumably because we are very aware of things changing, and everything needs to be broken down and dismantled to be built up in a better vibration. As healers and mediums, we try hard every day to ground and protect ourselves through meditation, but I think we are finding it hard to connect with our authentic self. Is there any advice that you can give us?"

V: "Each individual is on a different path. You must consider a meter with negative energy on one side and positive on the other, and we all are currently at a different position on this meter. You will find the average individual is currently positioned slightly towards the negative side and your journey must be always to return to the balancing point of this meter.

"Naturally, the more that energy is moved towards the negative side then further healing energy is required to return us to the balancing point. Fear, anger, and many other negative emotions contribute to this shift towards the negative side of the meter, so you must always try to keep your energy as balanced as possible. As fear and anger proceed in our lives, you will constantly find this more and more challenging."

S3: "Thank you."

V: "Your work with your trance guides will help you to achieve this. Never feel that you will fail as an individual, you understand? You cannot fail as an individual as this is impossible. However, there are individuals who are simply unsure of their path and are unwilling to see what's in front of them."

"You must choose a title for the book. You must have conversations. This is not an easy experiment that we bring forward for you. We are watching with great admiration for what you are trying to achieve here."

"I for one am grateful that I'm not there to experience this with you. It is a great pity that it has come to this. I cannot elaborate any further, as you will hopefully understand."

C: "Do you have any advice for the mediums here working in trance?"

V: "Only that you should try and ground yourself before commencing. You are working with physical energy brought forward from our dimension and to best experience this it is best not to open up to spirit beforehand as it can be overwhelming, but it is truly understandable if you do. And to my friend, it is a great feeling to be willing to help those in need and I would never criticise anyone for this, you understand?"

C: "Yes we do."

V: "There is a great healing energy in this room and it is very favourable with our friends in spirit. Everyone in this room blends well with our energies."

C: "Thank you once again for coming forward this evening. Please take our love and respect."

Summary – March 2023

ISAC commented that the trance medium who channelled CHRIS needed to ground themselves fully before commencing deep trance mediumship. This statement showed that specific conditions needed to be met at all times for this experiment to succeed, Nevertheless, the value of aiding a spirit person in need was also of a prime importance to the group and should never be underestimated.

ISAC reiterated that time doesn't exist in the spirit dimension, thus reemphasising that many of our questions concerning when certain events may or may not take place on Earth will seem irrelevant.

ISAC stated that we should always strive to be as balanced as possible in our lives and not let our energy meter stray too far to the negative or positive side. Therefore, it is of great importance that we experience events that induce emotions of both negative and positive persuasions in order to maintain a balanced perspective in life. ISAC commented that overcoming fear is the biggest challenge that we have to face, yet it is vital that we meet this head on as upcoming events will challenge us like never before.

Before this experiment began, I had suggested naming this book – 'The Great Awakening'. ISAC stated that we should have further conversations regarding a title for the book, which rather indicated that the title would be altered.

The current title was subsequently agreed just after the final session and we all felt it fits the book more appropriately.

Perhaps the most important information to come forward from ISAC was that we cannot fail as an individual, no matter how hard we try. This is a highly intriguing statement when you consider what is currently happening in our world and the stage in which we will undoubtedly find ourselves in within the near future. There will be individuals making decisions that will almost certainly have horrendous consequences for large amounts of people. Yet, ISAC states that these individuals are simply unsure of their path and are unwilling to see what's in front of them. This proclamation surely shows that regardless of any decision we make in the physical world, there is always an opportunity somewhere to alter the path that we find ourselves on, thus giving all lives more purpose and more challenges.

APRIL 2023

*The following transcripts were obtained on Thursday 13ᵗʰ April at The Stars from Above Sanctuary, Prestwick, Ayrshire, Scotland. Ten sitters, one co-ordinator, two trance mediums (**K & A**) and two trance guides (**The Blossom & CHRIS**) were involved in this session. The Blossom was the first guide to come forward.*

C o-ordinator (C): "Thank you for coming forward."
The Blossom (K): "It is my honour."
C: "Are you ready to accept questions from the sitters?

V: "Yes."

C: "Thank you. Would anyone like to ask a question?"

Sitter 1 (S): "Good evening my friend. The question I would like to ask is – as we are looking at this world and how these energies can change, to promote positivity many years ago we would have visions of the Virgin Mary or Fatima. Would anything like this happen this year?

V: "It is unlikely and the reasons are because, as you say going back in the past, these visions were given to people who were not as educated as you are here. Now that we can communicate directly to you in many ways, we would not so much require the vision of any of these reverend people that you speak of, but we would perhaps be able to guide you and to help you forward in a way that you understand. Those visions were used at a time when the human race took heed of them and it was such a miracle to them to have this, but your perception is so much more focussed now."

"Does that answer your question?"

S: "Yes it does."

V: "And you wish to ask more?"

S: "Yes if that's ok. You came through this evening and you reminded me of someone very close to me and my family and I just wanted to let you know that. Is that something that can happen at times?"

V: "The blend tonight requires the energy of each sitter here, so the vessel here is sitting in your energy, and in your energy is the energy of those that you love. They surround you and they are not very far from you. So, your perception of them is most accurate but each person here will perceive something slightly different, so you will all see people that you recognise because they are part of the universal energy of the spirit – and part of you."

S: "I would also just like to add that the lady who you reminded me of committed suicide – she was my step mum."

V: "May I add something? I know you have already discussed suicide in your group and its implications. It is important that you realise that although it is true that there will never be THE END, and that is correct, there is AN END to things and in order for a new beginning then sometimes it requires an end but it will never be THE end. Sometimes if there are too many things in the psyche or too many things causing pressure then it is time for an end so that there can be a new beginning."

S: "Thank you."

C: "Anybody else have a question?"

Sitter 2 (S2): "Good evening. I've been having disturbing dreams and visions of the Klu Klux Klan, but every hood worn by them is of a different colour. Could you please help me and tell me what the meaning of this is?"

V: "Dreams contain a lot of symbolic images and sometimes you will have to figure these out for yourself. Sometimes, I can tell you that they are linked to your spiritual journey, and perhaps in your past life or in your past journey – you have made such an encounter, but I would say to you that colour is always a positive thing and as a spiritual person you are aware how colour can enhance the human body. So, look to the colours and remember the brightest colour is your focus."

"Does that help my friend?"

S2: "Yes it does, thank you."

C: "Do you need a moment before we recommence?"

V: "No, I just think that someone is feeling unsettled but I'm not sure who. Let me just bring some harmony to the blend. Thank you, next question please."

Sitter 3 (S3): "I would like to ask a question. I have been getting information through about tsunamis. I know that there have been lots of tsunamis all over the world and I wondered if this is a danger that is getting closer to our lands here in the UK?"

V: "I understand your trepidation as you think of these as natural disasters but there are some analogies that we have used already with another discussion and we just wish to reit-

erate some of that. The Earth and the Spirit are very connected and we are here tonight to work with the Earth. Some
of the natural disasters are caused by the pressures applied to
the Earth. Sometimes they are the human kind of pressures
but also the Earth and the Spirit borrow energies from each
other and sometimes what happens is so-called natural disasters are just a way of the Spirit returning en masse so that the
energy can then be balanced. If you are afraid of the thought
of a tsunami then I would say that you must face your fear.
Do you understand this?"

S3: "Yes I do, thank you very much."

V: "Dip your toes in the water and they will go right
in."

C: "Thank you friend. Do you have any advice for the
next trance medium that will be attempting to bring forward
trance guides?"

V: "For the next person to sit as a vessel – I would say
that the most important thing for the vessel to do is to try to
relax and to still the mind and the thought, because the biggest bridge that we cross when we come to you is a troubled
mind, which can go into overdrive and cause a nervousness.
So, we just ask the vessel to try to relax as much as possible and enable the blend and the process that we have to go
through, so that it becomes a little bit easier for us. Therefore,
the vessel needs to relax more."

C: "Thank you. Should the co-ordinator (myself) help
with this?"

V: "Yes, I think it is always better to guide the medium down if they are nervous and this will help with their breathing, as you already know."

C: "Thank you. Are there any more questions?"

Sitter 4 (S4): "Are we ascending quicker than we were before?"

V: "No, we are all still in our own ascended journeys and there is no speed to it as we don't understand time in our world as life is infinite and it is just a matter of gathering knowledge and taking it back. But, I would just say to you that your time here is very precious and when you are here try not to waste the time, although as I said, we do not work with time in the spirit world, but in your world you have time here to make sure that you balance your thoughts. You will return here when it is time, do not worry about that and do not worry about the method of you leaving the spirit body behind and ascending because it will all happen in good time and there will be no rush to it. Each time you come back it will all be fine because you know that there is a little bit more to find and more to accumulate before you return, but you are all ascended souls and you have chosen to come here to gather more experience. So, while you are here, just try to experience as much as possible and also let go of fear as that will stop your knowledge. Fear is the most important thing that you must try to balance out and try not to get impatient or angry with yourself or with others as this will inhibit your accumulation of experiences and knowledge gained."

"Does this make sense to you?"

S4: "Yes it does."

C: "Thank you friend, may I also ask a question?"

V: "Yes, of course."

C: "When I wrote the book 'New Mediumship', which was written alongside spirit guides, I was informed that my spiritual level was that of a spirit guide (1ˢᵗ level of ascension in the spirit world), and that I had chosen to come back here to work rather than work as a guide in the spirit realm. Would that be a true reflection of everyone in this group, and do we all have someone here that we must guide before we return to the spirit world?

V: "I understand your question, but you must understand that you are not here to chaperone just one person – you are here to help lots of people awaken. There are many who slumber as we have said before and your aim or your task, or your mission if you like, is to make sure that each person you touch, you touch in a positive way. That is why we say not to be impatient, don't get angry, do not be fearful – because each time that you show people how relaxed, peaceful and harmonious you are in this life, then that affects them and that helps them to realise that there is more to fighting, there is more to anger, and that is your mission – and it's not just for one person but everyone."

C: "Thank you friend. Is this why this group has been assembled over the years – to bring this knowledge forth so that we have the opportunity to make this happen?"

V: "This group gathers here to give us in the spirit side and you on the human side an opportunity to blend together and to work together in this way. It takes a lot of energy and it takes people like you who are very spiritual in nature and is able to accept this way of communication. Some spiritual people do not like this way of communicating with us but this group is really good at receiving this and it is very natural to you, and we are very pleased with this. This is great progress for your group."

C: "Thank you friend, your kind words are much appreciated. We will try our best to work with you in a harmonious way, but you understand that we have fears at the moment of the direction the physical world is moving in and you will understand that as physical beings this will physically affect us in a different way than that of spiritual beings who will be able to view this differently. So, is there anything we can do in the physical world to help us get through what is about to transpire here?"

V: "What you can do is remember that you are a spiritual being that has been vacuum packed into a human body so you are much more than the human that walks this Earth – much, much more. If you fear what lies round every corner then you will not realise your full potential – and you are here to realise your full potential! So, you must not walk in fear and you must simply walk with confidence. You are confident because you are a spiritual being, and if there is an end or if something happens then it is just a step in your new beginning. Therefore, it is not THE end and it never will be."

C: "Thank you. We ask now that you return back to the spirit world and allow the trance medium to return back to the physical with our thanks."

V: "Indeed. I wish to tell you all that we honour and respect you, and we are so pleased with your progress. I wish you a good evening."

Co-ordinator (C): "Is the energy suitable for you friend?"

CHRIS (A): "The energy needs to settle first."

C: "Ok. Can you give us a moment?"

V: "Yes, please proceed."

C: "What we need to do folks is to send positive, loving, white light energy around this circle and then release it forward to the trance medium. To enable this, I would like all of the sitters to visualise white light emanating from the ceiling above and travelling down directly to the top of your heads, before then travelling down the chakras in your body - from the shoulders along to your wrists, before reaching the palms of your hands. Now feel the heat in your hands and when you feel ready please point the palms of your hands towards the trance medium and feel the energy being sent directly – from the ceiling above all the way to the source of our friends in spirit. Thank you.

C: "Is the energy now improving for you friend?"

V: "Yes."

C: "Good. You are most welcome to join us this evening and we are extremely privileged to have you with us. Are you able to answer questions from the group?"

V: "Yes."

C: "Thank you. Does anyone have a question?"

Sitter 5 (S5): "Good evening friend. I would like to ask a question to do with *man*. What is the most powerful aspect of *man* in the physical realm?"

V: "In my hands here is the most powerful thing for *man* and the energy that's just been sent is held here. That energy is with you wherever you go and anytime you feel in distress, or in fear, that energy is within you and that energy is shared with others. This energy is here. That's the power of *man*. This energy can be shared with others to help raise them, help hold them up, support… nurture… love… and it grows.

C: "Does that answer your question?"

S5: "Yes it does, thank you."

C: "Anybody else have a question?"

Sitter 6 (S6): "Can I ask a question please?"

C: "Yes you may."

S6: "It's about the hidden lies that's in our country, and particularly our government just now, can you explain the lies and what it's all about?"

V: "There are hidden lies for all of time and people focus on the hidden lies. There is always going to be lies and lies would not be lies if they weren't hidden. Lies are everywhere and it hides the focus from where it should be – on us. There are also hidden lies within ourselves that we don't face - lies that we don't hear and we choose not to see."

C: "Thank you friend. Some of us are having visions and dreams of conflict in our world. One was mentioned earlier – in reference to racial hatred. Is this racial hatred going to get worse, and is this the main reason why physical conflict in this physical world is going to get worse?"

V: "Racial hatred will become worse only if we each choose for it to become worse. It's a personal choice for each and every person. How that's perceived, like the hidden lies, will determine what you focus on and that's the eyes you will see through. There are always going to be some people who will have issues with racism and that's the choice they make when they partake in certain things."

C: "Thank you. Are there any other questions?"

Sitter 7 (S7): "Good evening my friend. This is more of a personal question. It's about the way I work with the spirit world and how things are changing. I feel that I need to get fitter for whatever's coming my way and as I am sitting here this evening I keep hearing 'Go on, go on', which I feel is relevant to this group. I'm also seeing a lot more shadows and I wondered how I should be communicating with those shadows?"

V: "Your eyes are opening to a bigger picture and it is telling you that there is something that you should be doing to look after your physical body. There are a lot of energies around you and you also see colours. There is also an element of your inner shadow as well and part of that is coming out to pinpoint you to look after yourself physically. As your eyes open to a bigger picture then you will find more and more that your own higher self is speaking to you through your intuition – and rightly so you should follow your intuition."

C: "Thank you friend. Can I ask you a quick question whilst the energy is still with us?"

V: "Yes please do."

C: "The vessel and I had a conversation before we commenced this evening. Will the vessel be continuing with the trance mediumship?"

V: "That will depend on the vessel's perception."

C: "Thank you for coming forward my friend; it's been an absolute delight."

V: "Thank you for the energy."

Summary – April 2023

Before the session began, the group discussed suicide and the fact that the rate of people choosing to end their existence here on the Earth had dramatically increased in recent times. The group wondered if this was due to a subconscious awareness of the impending global conflict and an unwillingness to experience such potential hardship and grief. The Blossom more or less confirmed this fact but emphasised that every end will always create a new beginning.

The Blossom spoke of tsunamis affecting our world as a possible result of energy transference between the Earth and the spirit dimension due to specific pressures. We were advised not to fear tsunamis but embrace them as a natural force and experience.

The Blossom mentioned dreams, and in particular the dream about the Klu Klux Klan, saying that dreams are mainly symbolic and will hint of a cryptic message. My own guide stated before this experiment began that we would all experience dreams of this ilk and our task was to find the hidden meaning behind them. This particular dream will remain private to the sitter who asked the question as we may all have a different perception of the hidden meaning here.

The Blossom made the comment that we are all spiritual beings that have been vacuum packed into a human body. This conjures the image of a highly pressurised being just waiting to be set free when the time is right to expand their knowledge.

CHRIS gave the powerful message that the greatest power known to *man* was held between the trance medium's hands. This energy had the power to heal, nurture, love, and support mankind. In that moment, the group truly felt the power of the spirit energy around us and the significance of an eternal lifeforce within all of us.

CHRIS commented that racial hatred will only become worse in our world if we so choose for it to become worse, thus emphasising that we all have personal choices and decisions to make, regardless of widespread opinion or belief. This suggests that we should all choose our own path and never follow mass collaborators or decision makers – particulary important when fear opens up divisions in society.

MAY 2023

*The following transcripts were obtained on Monday 22nd May at The Stars from Above Sanctuary, Prestwick, Ayrshire, Scotland. Eleven sitters, one co-ordinator, two trance mediums (**M & J**) and two trance guides (**Oephilia & ISAC**) were involved in this session. Oephilia was the first guide to come forward.*

Co-ordinator (C): "Thank you for coming forward friend. We know that you have been listening to our conversations and that you will wish to give us some guidance on what we discussed."

Oephilia (M): "Thank you for creating this opportunity for us to come through."

C: "Is the energy sufficient for us receiving questions this evening?"

V: "It is indeed."

C: "Thank you. Friend, we know you were listening to us earlier and you were aware of the meditation (with the journey and the guide). In the regards to the meter that was used in the meditation to gauge how positive or negative our energy levels currently are, can you please give us your thoughts on this?"

V: "It was interesting to hear you all talk about finding the middle ground of this meter (halfway between full positivity and full negativity). I was listening and I said to my medium when she was in a very deep meditative state – 'Go for the top one as you will have a whale of a time!' Then again, of course we can cope in that sort of time loop – the speed that it goes at. You are sensible, because when you are meditating you are coming into other realms, but the reality is that it is in your mind and your mind is experiencing it. Your mind is greatly affected by the fact that you live on a very concrete land."

"You see, it's very different to pop in and experience a little, as in reality the different levels are totally different because when you are experiencing things at the level where souls develop then you discover it is not a hierarchy – it is just natural. As spirits become more knowledgeable and mature then they are more able to cope with things. I hope that makes sense?"

C: "Yes it does."

V: "It's only sensible as you are always learning. On the earthly plane you will drive your vehicles, but you wouldn't just jump in the vehicle and put your foot down and drive to a hundred miles per hour. You have to learn slowly and through lifetime after lifetime. Eventually, all of you will be up to the 70's and 80's, or even the 90's (100 being total positivity) and we need people to have life experiences that will enable them to reach those levels. I don't know if that makes sense?"

C: "Yes it does, thank you, and it's a lot to think about there."

V: "Are there any more questions?"

C: "Can I just ask is this a different medium coming forward this evening? Is this a friend of mine who has worked through my own trance mediumship in the past?

V: "I have worked through this medium on a number of occasions, and as you know David, you have worked with many of the guides that work through this medium and we are spreading you all around."

C: "I understand, thank you. I am familiar with your voice and also the guidance."

V: "The thing is that when we come through different mediums, we are using a different physical body so therefore there will always be differences."

C: "Of course. Do you wish to use a different name for the purposes of the publication, or continue with the name Oephilia?"

V: "As I've said before, this particular medium does not need names – names are something that only people on the Earth plane require. We all know that we are you – and you are us and we all know each other."

C: "Absolutely, thank you. Does anyone have a question?"

Sitter 1 (S): "Tonight we were doing a meditation exercise and everybody was at different speeds and different numbers on the dials. Is there a reason for this?"

V: "There certainly is. You are all on different soul journeys and it is very dependent on how many different lifetimes on different planets and also different environments that have been experienced. It is also dependent on what you have learnt during those lifetimes, so just as on the Earth plane – you learn from what you experience. When you start to venture beyond, you carry those beliefs and values with you. You will sometimes meet someone who is a very young soul, regardless of their time spent on Earth, it might be someone in their late 60's but they may still be a very young soul. It really depends on how many lifetimes you've had and the experiences that you have repeated time and time again and not learned from, before eventually getting there. That is why as you do meditations then you will go to a level that you are able to comprehend and understand in order to assist you on your journey."

"Does that make sense to you?"

S1: "Yes."

V: "If you wish me to expand it in a particular way then please ask. As I said before, let me make it very clear, within spirit it is not a hierarchy. It doesn't mean to say that whatever level you soul is at is the right level for you and that doesn't make you any lesser or more than anyone else as we are all one and we all connect."

"Sometimes, what happens is that dreaded word - the 'ego', can become so destructive. We don't have ego but it is essential for learning on the Earth plane, and it is important that when you are sitting watching someone, whether it is on a mediumistic level or not, that you bear in mind that they are just the channel and it doesn't make them better than anyone else – because we are all as one. You are of us and we are of you. That is very important."

C: "Thank you for coming forward my friend and for guiding us with your wise words."

V: "Thank you to all of you present here. Without you, we are not able to come forward and communicate. Thank you one and all. We send you love, light and peace."

C: "Thank you."

Co-ordinator (C): "Thank you for coming forward my friend."

ISAC (I): "You are more than welcome."

C: "Is the energy sufficient for you to receive questions this evening?"

V: "Yes."

C: "Excellent, thank you. May I personally ask the first question please?"

V: "Yes."

C: "You were in the meditation earlier with the medium, I know this. What is your take on how that meditation went?"

V: "As you are aware, time is not a factor for us, but there are times when we allow immortals to be able to see the past, but never the future. We are more a movement where we can, as you would say, bend time. Time is very irrelevant where we exist, but for yourselves, it is an eternity."

C: "Thank you. As the regards to the meter in the meditation, would I be correct in saying that the guides would have the ability to move this, but are not allowed to?"

V: "As I have already said, time is irrelevant so movement of a meter is irrelevant."

49

C: "Okay, thank you. Does anybody have a question?"

Sitter 2 (S2): "Does the human race have new lessons to learn or are they just old lessons in a new time?"

V: "Every human being that is on the Earth plane has always a lesson to learn, whether it is of pure or evil origin, it will always be there. You have to remember that each individual is on your planet for a reason, whether it is to learn a lesson from the past, or to learn from their past."

C: "Does that answer your question?"

S2: "Yes thank you."

Sitter 3 (S3): "May I ask a question?"

V: "Yes, please do."

S3: "We are all very aware, that within the world at this present time, there is an awful lot of conflict. Has spirit activated individuals, for example Zelensky, and placed key people within the Earth in order to extend guidance to human beings through a very spiritual and highly developed individual?"

V: "We aren't allowed to interfere, as you are aware, but people are wakening up and asking questions within themselves. Smaller movements are gathering, a bit like people worshiping the sun and the moon, so as these smaller things happen then bigger groups will occur and more and more people may enter into this."

S3: "Can I just follow up with that question – as somebody that lives in this particular planet at the present time, I reflect back on people like Ghandi who appeared to have just arrived at a time that was essential for other humans to have that leadership and direction. That's why I was wondering if that was a pattern, or if it happens naturally – or if it was something that was influenced by spirit."

V: "Spirit influences nothing. Everything happens for a reason."

S3: "Okay, thank you."

C: "Anybody else want to ask a question?"

Sitter4 (S4): "It's regarding the question of time. I remember in a meditation being shown the past, the present and the future as being all combined. So, if we stay in the present then the future is already being created in the past. Would that be correct?"

V: "In a matter of speaking – yes. It depends on your one philosophy of time. Past, present, and future is as one."

S4: "So is that why we would always strive to be in the present?"

V: "Yes."

C: "Thank you friend. The vessel that you work with and me myself have been receiving visions of our future. Can I ask you please, are these visions coming from our own psychic ability or are these messages from guides or senior spirit people?"

V: "It's a combination of both – messages from our guides and the higher realms."

C: "Thank you. May I ask one last question? I don't expect an answer for this question, but I feel as if I need to ask this and I feel that you know I'm about to ask this – did spirit create mankind or did mankind create the spirit world?"

V: "That is one for you to think about yourself."

C: "The answer I expected, I appreciate that. Does anybody else have a question?"

Sitter 5 (S5): "On the Earth plane when humans produce children, sometimes they have twins or even triplets, and sometimes they all come from the one egg. In that situation, would twins or triplets all share the one soul?"

V: "No. The reason is that as an individual they are put on the planet for a reason so whether they are born in the same womb as 2, 3, 4 others, it is very irrelevant because it's a bit like chalk and cheese – you never get the same two, so therefore neither are the same nor differ in any aspect."

C: "Any other questions?"

Sitter 6 (S6): "It's a similar question to the last one as I have been made aware that as a soul we can choose to split and bring a percentage of our energy into multiple different lives at the one time as soul fragments. Would that be correct?"

V: "This may happen on the very odd occasion where a fragment of a soul may penetrate another one for a particular reason, but that is a decision that higher realm spirits will make – and only they can make that decision."

S6: "Thank you."

C: "Thank you my friend for coming forward. It's been an absolute delight. We ask that you go with our love and that you go with our respect. We hope to communicate with you again in the near future. Thank you."

Summary – May 2023

The group were taken on a meditation before this session and shown a meter that portrayed how they felt that the balance of our own personal energy was currently positioned at. The meter showed negative energy to the left, positive energy to the right, and naturally, the centre of the meter would be balanced perfectly.

Oephilia commented that in our meditations we would naturally feel that our energy was more balanced due to the fact that we had temporarily left the physical world and entered a subconscious state. The challenge would of course be to remain balanced in the physical world with all that was going on around us. Inevitably, we should all be able to remain balanced knowing that we can place ourselves in a meditative state whenever the pressures of modern-day living become too oppressive.

I asked ISAC the question about whether spirit created mankind or did mankind create the spirit world. This question surfaced due to a rather peculiar meditation where I was shown the future of our world and its inhabitants. The answer from ISAC was as expected due to the fact that our future is not as important as the present moment. All I would say in regard to the futuristic premonition is that artificial intelligence (AI) will play a hugely prominent part in our existence.

Isac also answered the question about my visions of the future by saying that it was a result of both a personal psychic awareness and also knowledge from our spirit guides. This would suggest that our future world is of some importance to the spirit world and may reflect on how our world is set up after the great awakening.

Isac then answered that our past, present and future are all but the one reality in a timeless motion. Perhaps the complexities of this situation are too far beyond our comprehension at this time. Maybe the reality is to just exist in the moment quintessentially.

JUNE 2023

*The following transcripts were obtained on Thursday 22nd June at The Stars from Above Sanctuary, Prestwick, Ayrshire, Scotland. Ten sitters, one co-ordinator, one trance medium (**D**) and three trance guides (**Gordon, Chung & ISAC**) were involved in this session. The questions were all prepared immediately prior to this session and all were asked by the co-ordinator.*

C o-ordinator (C): "Thank you for coming forward."
Gordon (D): "It is a great pleasure to once again be part of this wonderful experiment. It is my duty and my honour to welcome you this evening. Please be advised that I may morph into someone else or something else but do not be afraid as I am just your usual friendly spiritual being, coming forward to communicate with you this evening, trying to answer questions as best as I possibly can. Is this okay with everyone?"

C: "Yes, thank you."

V: "My indebted thanks to you all as you choose to spend some of your precious moments explaining the situation you find yourselves in. This group has been shortened this evening to suit the individual medium working in trance. We will be working with most of you in the coming months and we may take you out from this group now and again, as we have taken out some individuals this evening. This is not in any way a slight on anyone and if you are not here this evening then you may well return in the next meeting. You understand?"

C: "Yes we do,"

V: "There is much to be learned in this group and there is much to be learned on this physical planet that you dwell on at this precise time. Do not be alarmed about what you may read about here or see in your news programmes. There are way more individuals with a kind, gentle heart, than those who are sad and desperate in mind. You understand?"

C: "Yes."

V: "And if this world starts to crumble into chaos then it is because those with a kind heart foolishly started listening to those with a devious heart, as has happened in your past – and also in my past. I suffered such an enigma in my time on your Earth, when I was a small child. And at times, my parents would listen to what was being broadcast, yet not believe that things would take off in such a manner."

"There is not much you can do to affect others in the way they act or react. You can only take care of your own. You understand?"

C: "Yes".

V: "Because this is how you will judge yourselves when you return to the beautiful realms that you just visited in your meditations. There are those in the past who persuaded others to make wrong decisions and they are now finding themselves in a similar place, and it is not too late to make amends for their misdemeanours or simply wrong choices. Forgive me as I morph into another energy, as you may call it. One moment please…"

Chung (D): "You may ask your first question my friend."

C: "We were wondering about solar waves or solar flares, in particular the one's arriving in December. How will this affect us on the planet?

V: "Solar waves, or solar flares are natural occurrences, you understand?

C: "Yes."

V: "You ask if these will affect your natural world, your physical planet, I cannot answer this, my friend, but let me elaborate slightly. Do not fear what you do not understand. Does this answer your question?"

C: "Yes."

V: "Are you sure of that?"

C: "Yes, thank you"

C: "We have another question, which is about the Shumann Resonance. Why is it different this year and is it affecting our DNA?"

V: "You must please elaborate on what the term 'The Schumann Resonance' means to you."

C: "The electromagnetic energies that affect us.

V: "Schumann is just the individual here. There are significant differences with electromagnetic energy from the physical being and the being which communicates with you now. This significant difference in the energy of the higher vibrations will not affect the energies within the spirit world. However, it may affect the energy in the physical planet which of course covers your Earth plane. However, this change in your planet's energy pales into insignificance compared to the energies stored in every single individual living on your planet. It is a complicated matter as the question doesn't really exist to us. People's energies are much more affected by other people's energies than natural occurrences in our environment."

C: "Okay, we will think about that one."

V: "In an essence, what is expected doesn't always affect reality."

C: "Our next question concerns the water tables – the water in the Earth below the ground. Is something currently affecting this, and is too much being taken and affecting the balance?"

V: "It is a good question. The problem is overpopulation in your planet, and what you may refer to as seasonally afflicted weather conditions. You see, water is unique. Do you know where water comes from?"

C: "The clouds? The sky? The rain?"

V: "Yes, but where did water originate from in the Earth?"

C: "We don't know."

V: "Indeed, nobody really knows how it arrived here."

C: "I suppose it's a bit like the chicken and the egg?"

V: "Indeed. Measurements of water are affected by consummation. And if you have too many consumers then naturally your water tables will be affected."

C: "So, as humans, we are wasting water?"

V: "Indeed. And without water you cannot feed. And if you do not feed… you cannot exist here. But do not fear, this will be taken care of, but for now, this issue will get gradually worse. Question number 4 please?"

C: "This question is about crop circles. Who or what is responsible for the most recent one's as they are different geometric shapes? Is this to bring in a different vibration or frequency?"

V: "We know that there are many differences of opinions in your world regarding these incidents. And there are differences of opinions in this group also, am I correct?"

C: "Yes."

V: "There are some who think this is the work of those from another planet, and there are those who believe it is the work of ingenious human beings. In fact, it is neither. I'm afraid I cannot elaborate any further."

C: "Is that along the lines of how the pyramids came into existence?"

V: "Perhaps."

C: "Is it a natural occurrence?"

V: "Indeed."

C: "Does it bring frequencies with it?"

V: "Indeed."

V: "You think of the tree. When the tree is in full bloom you can hardly see the branches below the leaves, but when the leaves fall off then the branches become much more visible and the tree takes on a much different shape and appearance – almost lifeless in comparison. What causes these circles to be created? Perhaps they were always there. Perhaps you are only seeing them through your naked eye. Perhaps you are only seeing them when, like the tree, they are in full bloom."

C: "So it's about perception?"

V: "Not just perception, my dear. It is very much reality."

C: "You mean that we need to see things more clearly without judgement or bias, after the fog has lifted, so to speak?"

V: "Perhaps, my friend."

C: "We are awakening?"

V: "Perhaps, my friend."

C: "That leads us on to our next question."

V: "One moment, my friend."

Gordon (D): "May I congratulate you on a phenomenal set of questions received this evening. You really have tested the minds of those who wish to offer you guidance and advice. The difficulty is just exactly what we can or cannot elaborate on. Not so much that we cannot give you advice, but the answers may not be totally understood. There are reasons for this – you need to have the tools and the know-how to break down the calculations before being aware of the solutions. So, the answers we give may be rather obscure and at times seem flippant. Does this make sense?"

C: "Yes it does."

V: "Your recent crop circles could not be created by a physical being, although they could be replicated by humans. This is a subject that puzzled me for a long time when I was on Earth. I used to ask my guides questions about pyramids and other natural creations that we could not work out how they were created, and the interesting thing is there is always a reason why these phenomena's occur. Yet, it is not always clear how they could be here. Feel free to ask your own guides about this subject during your meditations. The last thing I will say is that the creation of the circles is of no great importance to us or indeed to your yourselves, so don't worry if the question remains unanswered in your physical lifetime. As a spirit person, I could technically create one of these circles outside of this room as we speak. In fact, I could make objects disappear and reappear at the click of your fingers. You understand now?"

C: "Yes."

V: "Does this now answer your question?"

C: "Yes it does. Would you like the next question?"

V: "Indeed friend, before I morph into another being again. There is a friend here who wishes to come forward and answer some questions… but I am keeping him at bay!"

C: "We look forward to asking him the next question."

V: "He may be needed as he is of a much higher vibration."

C: "Well, when you were talking earlier about vibrations, or how we see things and perceive things, I think that leads on to the question we have about the 5th dimension. Humanity, as a whole, how far along are we in that evolution and how can the vibration be held in our human form?"

V: "May I congratulate you on this question. This question proves how well this group is developing. It also answers the question why you are here with us this evening. When you talk of 5th dimension then you must realise that we are all in the 5th dimension at this meeting. It is only gravity that prevents this from being permanent, you understand?"

C: "Yes."

V: "You talk of time but time is not required and there is no need in the 5th dimension to calculate such a force. There is much that we cannot say but more will become clear in your lifetimes. Your vibrations are affected by gravity, but our vibrations are much higher and unaffected. You already know this."

C: "We are grounded then?"

V: "Indeed, our vibrations don't react like the vibrations on the physical planet. Our science is much more developed. Our vibrations do not travel in just one direction, they travel everywhere. The resonance you spoke of earlier creates a loop and every soul is part of this loop. The higher the dimension – the purer the energy develops in the loop, whereas the lower energies are governed by the science of physicality, and your atomic structure. You speak of Schumann's Resonance but this does not exist in our vibration, only the physical. We may be separated in structure but not in lifeform. You will read in your books of many dimensions and your meditations will take you through those different dimensions. This is not something you will immediately be aware of since you will be able to vibrate into anything, but always remaining where you feel most comfortable. You understand?"

C: "Yes."

V: "If you go to the highest vibrations and feel that this is not your place, then you will choose to remove yourself. This won't be the choice of other energies – but your own choice to do so. This is a natural choice and feeling. You have another question?"

C: "You said that you vibrate in many directions. Is that what timelines consist of and being able to move through timelines?"

V: "They are not timelines my friend but you are, in a way, assuming correctly. To vibrate you leave the past and move to the future in your physical state. Vibration to us is like oxygen to you. To us, it is not physical motion – it is simply existence. Our atomic energy works in this fashion."

C: "We have a few more questions. I will try and pick out one that is relevant to what we have been talking about. Can I ask, do you as a trance guide know all that is to come, and if so then why don't you reveal specifics?"

V: "Yes, we have inside knowledge to what is occurring in your time force, and we have the ability to read one's thoughts so we know everything. We have the influence to change these thoughts, but if we were to do so then it would change the outcome. If we gave you an insight to these issues then it would also change your thoughts."

C: "Is it also because actions that look very predictable can change very rapidly through the actions of someone on the Earth plane?

V: "Very much so. It is simply cause and effect. There are things that we can do or are allowed to perform. For example, there are one or two souls in this group that do things for us, but this is very rare. We must retain the ability to learn by ourselves but we sometimes send some souls back to Earth that we hope will work for us. This is not us sending humans back – this is us sending like-minded guides back – you understand?"

C: "Yes."

V: "It is like my good self, returning to the physical dimension. I would blend with the physical and you would not know. This is why we give clues to what may happen. We put the questions in your minds so that when you ask them and then receive the answers, it gives the impression that you have found the solution to the problem yourselves. If we gave you all the answers and simply told you what was happening then you would have no reason for being here. There would be nothing to learn because you would be aware of every-thing before you came. You could prepare for everything and this would be against the learning experiences that we use to progress through our realms."

C: "Thank you. You have given us lots to think about tonight."

V: "You may find that I've given you very little, my friend. Perhaps you all have the answers within your domains. All I have really done is confirm these suspicions."

C: "Do you have any advice for us as a group, or circle, how we can help the development of the book?"

V: "Continue what you have been doing, my friends. You are doing a marvellous job. Your commitment is fantastic. The medium is most pleased with all of you."

C: "We have a question regarding hybrid souls. What exactly are they, and would you be able to tell us more about what their role is?"

Chung (D): "This is a question that I knew would be asked this evening. Hybrid souls have been written about in the past – but termed as soul fragments. Soul fragments have been thought of as pieces of soul that have been drifted into this individual or that individual, but this is not necessarily true. Let's say for example you have a physical vessel and a soul transcends into this physical vessel – this in essence becomes a hybrid soul. It takes the brain to give the human element and the soul for the spiritual facet, thus creating a hybrid soul. However, the soul may alter format from the present incarnation to a previous incarnation (you might refer to this as a past life) and this creates what we would term as soul fragments. So, an individual from the past becomes a soul fragment hybrid transcending into the human brain of this animal. The important thing to realise is that it is many fragments of just the one soul, rather than fragments of many different souls. You may witness this change in a soul as simply mood swings in people. You may awaken in a bad mood but we would term this as an alternative soul fragment in a hybrid state. Imagine energy from the past choosing to incarnate on a specific day, then altering to a different fragment on the next day. The difficulty here is that if many soul fragments from the same period of your past transcend at the exact same time then potentially you could be opening up Pandora's Box. In your current time limit – this will happen. Questions?"

C: "Is that why we currently have so many suicides?"

V: "Partly, my dear. Partly. Suicides are an individual decision and not all individuals choose this method of passing to spirit, but it is a major factor. You must understand that every soul has the ability to sense what will be coming in your physical future. This sense of impending doom may affect the particular soul fragment from the past to such an extent that they simply cannot face themselves. You understand? They cannot face themselves and this becomes too much for them, resulting in that hybrid soul choosing to prematurely end this existence."

C: "So the soul has chosen to come to the Earth plane to relive an experience of a past life, but in the process they cannot conclude this, so therefore end it?"

V: "In many cases, yes."

C: "So therefore, do they have to repeat the experience again?"

V: "Almost certainly on all occasions, with the odd exception. There are many who have been deliberately sent here on a specific mission. When this mission is cut short, you cannot develop internally – but it is always your decision. If this is an experience that you cannot break free from then it is advisable to ask for another mission."

C: "Does that mean that another soul can then use that physical vessel if the existing soul wants to leave?"

V: "No, as that vessel would be retired."

C: "Okay, thank you."

V: "A new physical vessel would need to be… as you say… born."

C: "I understand."

V: "A new physical vessel would need to be born, and the soul fragments would have the ability to manipulate this new vessel. If you have issues with the past then you will bring that fragment through when your time is correct. You will make this choice each and every one of your days. The individuals in this group have the ability to remove fragments temporarily during your 24-hour day. You can do this through meditation. Now I will tell you something that will make you understand this subject better. When you return nightly to spirit in your dream state, you will meet up with your elders and you will decide which fragment will come forward on the next of your physical days. If you sense impending doom – then your souls fragment will be the one that has to deal with that situation. You understand?"

C: "Yes. When you talk about reliving an experience, is it the experience you relive or is it the lesson learned? We ask this, because if you have not learned to be compassionate then that could be learned through different experiences. So, is it the lesson that you come back to relearn or is it a specific experience?"

V: "It is a complicated question, my dear. The medium has written a book all about this and the explanation will be better from the book than it will be from me. But let us just say that you have the opportunity to learn from experiences in the physical world when you return to the spiritual realms. If this is not achieved in the spirit realms then you may wish to come back to the physical. You cannot relive this experience in the physical world – only in the spiritual realm. This is because the spirit realm has no timeframe; therefore, you can revisit this exact experience over and over again in your eternal consciousness. If you returned to the physical world then you would only be able to relive a similar experience that has still to take place in order to see how you react to it this time."

C: "Can I just ask, in regard to some of these experiences that you are talking about, it sounds like a hybrid soul is living in a negative situation, however if that hybrid soul in the physical experience for the second time round then behaves in a more positive way, then wouldn't that be a huge improvement for society?"

V: "Indeed."

C: "But whereas if that soul was a bit of a tortured soul, and in a position of power, could that individual then be in a position to create a mass suicide within society?"

V: "These are possibilities my friend, but as we discussed earlier the meter is weighted heavily in the positive at this stage and there are many more souls reliving experiences that will benefit them. But at some point in your physical time – think of the solar eclipse – the light suddenly goes out completely on a very rare occasion, and this may happen with you. And, at that point, we are powerless to act. We must let the natural progression occur. You have one last question?"

C: "Actually, we have two questions. The first question is - why are lay lines moving?"

V: "This is a question that does not need answered as you can never stand still. Your world continually revolves and everything in it continually moves. Lay lines are not as important as you may think they are. They are energy fields – part of our energy, but they do not vibrate as much as you do, or I do."

C: "Thank you. The final question concerns the quest that we are on just now and what the group is hoping to achieve. How do you feel it is going and is there enough here for us to make a book?"

V: "One moment please."

ISAC (D): "Good evening. We would not be here if this was the case. The group is progressing as we would wish. We will make changes at your meetings. We will bring in new energies and remove certain ones – just to keep the balance correct. Normally this would be done by the circle leader, but we have been given permission by the circle leader to act on his behalf. We will take charge of this. The importance of this publication should not be underestimated. We will endeavour to ensure that every piece of information is of relevance and when everything has been collated then we will work with the medium to structure the book in a way that we intend it to be. We wish to thank every one of you for your wonderful energy and your commitment to this project. This is a unique experience and it will never be replicated."

Summary – June 2023

Just before the meeting in June I was asked by my trance guides if I would take over the trance mediumship for this particular session. It was a bit of a surprise but I knew that the guides had a good reason for this and I was happy to go along with whatever they had planned.

I was further informed that the guides wished the sitters to prepare questions beforehand so that more depth could go into them. The group then discussed what questions to ask whilst I meditated in another room so that I wasn't aware of what would be asked.

As a result, some extremely well thought out questions were presented to my guides – Gordon Higginson, Mr Chung & ISAC.

Gordon said that the upcoming conflict in our world reminded him of when he was a child during the second world war. He did not give any more detail concerning this comparison but did say that a concerning situation would arise due to people with kind hearts being misled by those with devious ones.

Mr Chung stated that there would be a shortage of water in our world due to overconsumption. We can only assume that our weather will inevitably contribute to this shortfall. Nevertheless, Chung also said that this predicament would be taken care of, which hinted at the spirit world somehow coming to our rescue.

Chung was asked if he knew specifically what was about to occur on our planet that would drastically affect our way of living and he confirmed that he did. However, he further alluded that if he informed us of all of the facts then our thought patterns may change and this would almost certainly affect the outcome.

Chung commented that the guides occasionally send back souls that are prepared to work for them in important matters. It is unclear if these chosen souls are here simply as just observers or are actively influencing the way our world develops. It is clear though that despite the trance guides having the ability to change the way the people of our world behave; they cannot directly get involved in this process as life on Earth would suddenly become much more premeditated and predictable.

ISAC stated that when the last recording has been made and documented that he would be working with myself to summarise all that has been written. I hope that my small part in this process will do justice to the eventual publication and ensure that nothing is ever underestimated.

JULY 2023

*The following transcripts were obtained on Monday 18th July at The Stars from Above Sanctuary, Prestwick, Ayrshire, Scotland. Five sitters, one co-ordinator, two trance mediums (**K & M**) and two trance guides (**Jules & Gordon**) were involved in this session. Jules was the first guide to come forward.*

Co-ordinator (C): "Good evening friend, how are you this evening?"

Jules (K): "Just settling with the energy, is that okay?"

C: "Absolutely. We know there is some noise outside of the room but this is moving on shortly."

V: "Yes, that is okay and is to be expected. How are you all this evening?"

C: "We are all good, thanks."

V: "You may think that the group is small but don't be deceived as it is very large. Each of you brings much energy with you and you bring all of your little spiritual teams together and this makes this room full. There are many, many, here and we all work in the light. And in the light, we only work in the truth, and our aim is to be honest with you tonight. All of you work to the best of your ability – in the truth and in the light. But we understand that you are a human kind and that you are working in a human existence, and sometimes things can get a little bit distorted during your many encounters with others, and sometimes you lie a little to yourselves and to others, but we ask you to strive for the truth. Sometimes the honesty can be hurtful – so please do not be hurtful. Be pure of heart."

"For those who do not understand the truth of the light, as you do, they feel that this is a challenge to them as they are challenged by your light. The truth is a challenge to those who live in a lie. And when I say those who live in a lie, by this I mean that they slumber. So, they need some inspiration – like 'the dragon is awake' – this doesn't mean that it will be flying around the room breathing fire – it is just an expression. I warn you all that there is no need to be afraid. By that we just mean that sometimes people would just let the dragon sleep for they are afraid. But there is no need to fear as it is done in love and in truth. Do not be afraid to poke the dragon awake for it means you know harm."

"It is very quiet now. We have sent a quiet whisper around the room and we wish to say to you that we are very honoured to be here with you all and it is also our privilege to be here too, and to blend in the energy of the people sitting here is indeed something very, very special to us. We are very, very aware that it takes a lot of your energy and your time, and that sometimes things do not seem to be in alignment, but please be assured that they are perfectly aligned."

C: "Friend, thank you. We spoke earlier in the group discussion about preparing questions in advance for the trance guides but I was subsequently told by my guide to just get on with it. Is that okay with you? Can we just individually ask you questions?"

V: "Yes, I think sometimes when you are asking for questions that some are finding it quite difficult to come up with anything due to the human thought process. Some of the answers to the questions actually lie within you, so these are normally the questions that bubble to your surface – and you all know the answers already. This results in you thinking that we are being cryptic with you – but we are not. We are mainly letting you look into yourselves, because you have so much more than you think. And you think that sitting before you is an oracle to answer all of your questions, when you yourself are an oracle. You have many, many of the answers within you, and some of the answers are not really suitable for the question. Does that make sense to you?"

C: "Yes, absolutely."

V: "It is merely that we have a limited amount of your time to speak to you and sometimes it is just time for us to go with the flow – and this is a good way to work, because sometimes when we are aligning the energy up and you are trying to accumulate some information, then it can get lost. Does that make sense?"

C: "It does thanks."

V: "If you don't mind, I would like to speak a little bit about energy. Our team here, and your team, are working very much together on the Earth plane, and it is our goal to make the Earth a better place. We look upon the Earth as being a living energy, or a living being if you like, and all of you are living here in this energy field. You are both human and you are also spirit – but mainly living a human existence and you must be mindful of this human existence within the being that is the Earth. The purpose is to keep this Earth alive and to keep it healthy. This is why we come back and forward because we are always working on involving human-kind so that it merges with the spirit kind to do the best that we can when on the Earth plane."

"There are many times when the experiment, or the formula, is not quite right, and we have to go back to the drawing board and start again with some things, but you are always presenting yourselves in the best way possible when you are representing spirit here on the Earth plane. For we are very much beholden to the Earth plane for the energies that are here; we need the Earth because it contains a blend that we require for part of our existence in the spiritual realms. There are many other factors involved and our mission is to enhance the energies of the Earth plane and to make sure that we are doing the very best that we can. You understand this?"

C: "Yes."

V: "So when we come here and you ask a question and then we give you the answer, we are not asking you to follow what we say, or do as we say, we are merely giving you advice. We are merely giving you something that may help you – but as always, the answer lies within you. The intent lies within you. So, work on your truth; work on your love, and always with the light – that is all that we request from you."

"We do not give you orders; we do not give you things to do, we merely ask that you do the best that you can with the path that you have made for yourself before you arrived on the Earth plane. Each of you here decided that you wanted to come here and help – and you are helping. It's just that we have to wake the slumbering dragon in you. You are very much aware that there are vast energies on this Earth – some are chaotic and you must stand your ground when you are here. You must stay strong and face adversity, and always with the best of intentions, always with the love, and the truth. Honour each other and do not forget that people who challenge you are simply not as awake as you, and they do not realise that they are putting obstacles in your path. It is not their intention to do this, but then, you do not always want things to be too easy as life is to be lived and we need to experiment and experience many things when we are here. Do no harm to each other when you are here. You may begin to ask questions."

C: "Thank you friend. We have a couple of questions regarding the upcoming publication. The first one is regarding your identity. Do you wish to use the same identity as before i.e. The Blossom?"

V: "We have an agreement for this energy that you may identify as 'Jules'. There is a little background if you would like me to elaborate?"

C: "Certainly, thank you."

V: "My time on the Earth plane, I was very much an alchemist. I was always experimenting as I was fascinated with the Earth and I was travelling around a lot. I was fascinated by things like gravity and other scientific things. I did many, many experiments and spent a long time on my own. When I was returned to spirit, I found that I was an ascended soul because of my work with the Earth. I then joined a team and through this I have continued my experiments and now have a better perspective of it and I am now able to do so much more from this plane here than when I was on the Earth plane. I was always very fascinated by the scientific ways and I was also very fascinated by the cycles on Earth. The earth moves in cycles – not so much in straight lines, but in cycles. So, every day you have cycles, every season you have cycles, moon cycles – these are the things that the Earth endures and this was my fascination, amongst other things. I hope that answers your question?"

C: "Yes thanks, that opens up a vast pallet for our imaginations. When I was typing up the notes from our previous meeting, I have had to alter some of the grammar that was brought forward from the guides due to my perception that it wasn't quite suitable for public consumption and I had to change one or two words, is this okay with the spirit team to do this?"

V: "You will know yourself that when you are compiling your transcripts that we are with you."

C: "Yes I felt that was the case."

V: "We will correct anything that needs amending, because sometimes when we are coming through the medium there are slight distortions in the vocabulary and other little nuances, and this is perfectly fine as long as you are not interfering."

C: "Yes, I felt as if someone was telling me to change certain words, thank you for confirming this to me. Can I ask the sitters if anyone has a question for Jules please?"

Sitter 1 (S1): "Could I just ask please, are sprit quite happy with where we are and where we are progressing with this quest?"

V: "Happy, is not a word that we often use in the spirit realms, but we are always watching the progress and we understand that there has been a little step back the way for some, but that is alright. Things are moving at a pace that suits the group and we are happy for this. What you may find in the next coming chapters of the book is that things will move much more quickly. You will see that there will be a faster pace, is that okay?"

S1: "Yes, that is good, thank you."

C: "Anybody else have a question?"

Sitter 2 (S2): "Can I ask a question, please?"

V: "Yes, certainly."

S2: "Like you, when I was in meditation earlier, I also witnessed a dragon. The dragon showed me destruction and fire, but it also showed me what looked like a rebirth. We mentioned earlier, viruses killing them off, so is this a way of Mother Nature raising the temperature in the world?"

V: "Fire is a great cleanser if you think of the phoenix rising from the ashes. Fire, although it is synonymous with destruction, is a movement of energy and also a way of cleansing. You may look at the burning forest and see that fire has burnt away all of the trees but you cannot stop the growth. Perhaps there was a need for all of this to be burnt away. Anything that happens like this on the Earth plane, I have to reiterate that it won't be dragons that are responsible for this. We have just given you the analogy of the dragon - of the cold-blooded beast, that slumbers, being awakened to breathe fire. That is to say that within all of us, there is the ability for destruction – but not all destroyers are necessarily destructors. Again, we give you some critique."

S2: "Is that why they were showing me 50-60 degrees centigrade and parts of southern and northern Asia?"

V: "That is for you to figure out. You will not be getting everything on your plate. You must know that sometimes the things that are in your meditation are things that you may already be thinking of; sometimes the things in your meditation are things that we like to introduce to your thoughts. Does that make sense to you?"

S2: "Yes, I think so."

C: "Jules, can I ask a question, please?"

V: "Yes, please do."

C: "You stated that you were fascinated by science and alchemy etc. when you were on the Earth plane. In the physical world of medical science, we have a gland in the human body called the pineal gland. This gland is responsible for releasing melatonin to help us sleep, but in my experience, it is also responsible for affecting adrenaline in my body that enables me to blend with spirit energy. My question then would be, is this gland as vital to spirit energy as it is to physical energy to ensure we can both communicate with each other?"

V: "The whole of the physical body connects with the energies from the spirit world. There are parts of the body that we connect easier with, but we connect with the whole of the human body, that is why we are involved in the birth of more evolved super-humans. These humans will have an increased capacity in the brain power and the mind and we both connect with the entire human system. It is no coincidence, that in the past, humans have had higher powers and they have made new scientific discoveries. That is because of their enhanced brain power that we were able to connect with them and able to guide their thoughts. This is very much an evolved state of being. We connect through all parts of the body, that is why you can feel us coming through your solar plexus and other parts of your human system. You will feel us all around you as we can connect with the whole of you. You understand?"

C: "And will these 'super humans' appear after the fire has ravaged the Earth or before?"

V: "They will not be classed as super humans because evolution on Earth is a process that takes time, but we are working very closely with this process, and there are many here in this room that can connect very well with the spirit world. You already know that when your body dies and you move to the spirit realms that it will be in an ascended place because you have already been here and you will simply return home with some more information and some more relevant pieces of the puzzle, if you like, that we are constantly working on. Each new human being that is born on the Earth plane shall have a little bit of enhancement that is always being worked on, so as they grow in their human body, they will become more aware of us at a much quicker rate. You understand?"

C: "Yes, very interesting."

V: "The evolution of the humankind is tied to the evolution of the spirit."

C: "Thank you."

V: "I will leave you now."

C: "Thank you Jules for coming forward. Please stay nearby for the rest of the evening."

V: "I will not be far."

C: "Thank you very much for your wonderful energy."

Gordon (M): "Welcome to you all."

C: "Thank you friend for coming forward."

V: "We meet again."

C: "Yes. Can I ask who comes forward for identification purposes please?"

V: "I think you know, David, who comes forward."

C: "Thank you very much sir, for coming forward, it is a great honour for us to be here with you this evening. We are very much obliged that you have given us your energy. May we ask some questions please?"

V: "You may."

C: "Does anybody have a question for Gordon?"

Sitter 3 (S3): "At the end of this book session, what will happen to this trance group?"

V: "That depends very much on what you wish to do next. We are not going to come forward and put things on a plate for you. You must communicate and then make decisions, some of you will go forward and some of you won't. You are all developing at different levels and I have to say that sometimes it is good to have a good shake up and let the dust off, before starting again under a new mentor and leadership. You are all where you are meant to be as that is the nature of your contract that you have taken. You see, you often wish to have all the answers, but we don't give you the answers - because as my colleague said earlier - humankind ask for advice when they already know the answer but it's not necessarily the answer they want. So, they hope that someone else gives them another option. Does that make sense?"

S3: "Yes, thank you."

V: "You will be where you are meant to be, you are all on the right path. Do not be too blinkered as there are many paths that lead to where you need to be. Does anyone else wish to ask a question?"

Sitter 4 (S4): "Can I ask please, could you give us a date as to when all this chaos and anarchy in our world will come to an end?"

V: "That is very difficult to answer. It really depends on how you define chaos and anarchy. The reality is that there has always been chaos and anarchy. Humans get so tied up but all we all we want you to do is to be human in the moment – be here now and stop worrying about what may or may not happen. All that matters is that when something happens – how do you then react? The frustration it causes us, hearing you thinking if this or if that, if maybe, instead of just stopping and enjoying the moment that you are in. You can't do anything about what's happened in your past. There are also very few things you can change in your future. All that you can do is build on the light. Create the light that will help this world to become a kinder, more loving, and supportive place. I can say no more than that. I'm just still smiling about your perception of chaos and anarchy. You want to be on this side! Hah, we have fun and games too. I know that there is a genuine fear, but on a more serious note – fear is nothing, it is only what you allow it to be. Can you change it? Can you spend hours worrying about it while your life passes you by? Look for the light, build the light. When you see someone in need, or see someone sad, a smile or a gentle word will build the light. That will make people who are slumbering – like the dragon that was mentioned earlier – wake up. That is what this is all about. It is to waken all those that have allowed themselves to become wrapped in negativity, unable to enjoy this very special time that you have on this Earth planet. Does that make sense to you?"

S4: "yes it does, thank you."

V: "Thank you. Any other questions?"

Sitter 5 (S5): "Is the energy that's surrounding our planet affecting our children in a negative way?"

V: "It's affecting the adults, which in turn affects the children. So, the reality is that whatever energies you put out, or whatever thoughts you put out, are returned to you. If you are living in a negative way then you will find that children are the most perceptive amongst humankind. They hear conversations which are misinterpreted, thus creating another spiral of anxiety. Unless you are very careful, you are just creating constant circles, going round and round and round. Because of the complexity of your world and because children are developing at a much faster rate, you will have to be very careful of the environment that is being created for them. Do not raise the children to be afraid. I repeat again… fear not! Fear is only as strong as the power you give it. I hope that helps?"

S5: "Yes, thanks."

V: "It all comes back to what they experience, and adults have a responsibility for whatever children are exposed to."

C: "Gordon, can I ask where you are in the spiritual realms just now? I know that when you passed to spirit that you joined up with Chung or Choo Chow as he is known to others, are you now blending in a higher energy? Are you ascending the spiritual ladder or are you remaining where you started so that you can work with trance groups? Or is it just soul fragments of yourself that comes forward here as your main energy force transcends into a higher vibration?

V: "The spirit team blend with many, many mediums on the Earth plane. Some work at very high levels, but there are a lot who don't necessarily need to be at that stage of development. We see where the need is and that is where we go. We work in teams, but those teams work with other individuals in this room. Our quest on your side is to basically go where we are needed, and yes most of the time we are functioning at a higher level. We will always work with mediums that are working with no ego and are working purely in the light, with love and with trust."

C: "Thank you, and if the medium isn't working with all of those attributes, will you not work with them?"

V: "We would guide them, but in all honesty, we need to find channels that are going to be very effective in order for us to be able to get the information through that is required, so that hopefully people become more aware of the spiritual side of life. As you all go out and share in the light and spread your light, and the little candle in the corner brightens up so that people can start to see that light, you will still be aware of people's depressive state – but all that's really needed is a bit of light. The answer doesn't have to have huge implications as sometimes it's just the little steps that count. Does that make sense?"

C: "Yes."

V: "Is there anything else you wish to ask?"

V: "It's fascinating as we can actually see you all. The medium's eyes do not need to be open. There is always a quiet one in the room who may want to ask something yet does not ask it. There is no fear in asking a question."

Sitter 6 (S6): "Okay, can I please ask about an experience I had recently. I was shown that electronics are going to be switched off all over the world. Now, I'm not a fatalist, but I was wondering if this was a vision showing me humankind being brought back to basics. It was like being shown a tsunami in our world that was causing widespread chaos, which was unusual for me as I don't usually see negative things in my mind. My question then is, did I really see this in my mind or was I being shown something cryptic?"

V: "In a sense, there is a sort of tsunami going on around your world. But that tsunami, as I said previously, is fear. Once fear manages to get into the little corners of your mind and you find yourself blending or mixing with other individuals who have a similar, negative thought pattern, then fear will multiply incessantly. I believe my colleague was speaking to someone earlier about how they would interpret a dragon's flames as being destructive. So, what I'm saying is that perhaps when you get some of these images coming into your head then just stop, pause for a moment, and then just think.

We are so open you see, we are open to spirit, but we are open to people that you come across during the day that makes you feel quite chirpy or quite angry. You don't always realise how many external happenings, events or energies intrude into your energy, so just be aware. I don't know whether that helped?"

S6: "Yes, it did."

V: "One thing, I think, that mediums are always doing is questioning – Is it them, or is it me? We don't tend to bring fear to you. We might alert you by giving you a prompt if you were in a vulnerable place. We might give you an instinctual feeling that something needs attended to, but we would not bring you fear. Is that making any sense to you?"

S6: "It does thanks."

V: "Thank you,"

C: "We were previously given a date by the spirit team, in April of this year, when something significant would happen that would hint at what was about to come. Is there another date between now and the end of the year that you could give us that would give us a further clue as to what is going to transpire? Perhaps a date in November of this year?"

V: "Let's be blunt, anything could happen in November. Let us look at the past week and how many significant things happened. The problem you will have is that what appears to be inevitable within the Earth plane can change very quickly by the actions or the non-actions of any individual. So, yes things could happen but we are not going to prophesize or say on such and such a date that this will happen. Lots of things may happen, but lots of things happened in the last month. If you look closely, it might not be affecting us personally, but if you look at some of the events happening all over your world – for those people that is majorly stressful. It is, how do you say, part of humankind to always be looking for troubles to seek. We would say to you to accept each day, and whatever comes forward will be judged on how you react or respond, and that's the important thing. So I'm sorry but I'm not going to give you a date because between now and then I have no doubt that there will be many places in this world that experience dreadful, dreadful things, because as we sit here observing your area of this Earth plane, we float all over your world and I can assure you that major significant things are already happening every day as we speak. All things change – it is part of the energy of the planet and the interactions that human beings have with each other within this planet. This is why you come to this planet – to learn, before coming home to share your experiences, put it into the knowledge base and see where it takes you next."

C: "Thank you, Gordon. We know in the spirit realms that you have a duty not to interfere with what happens on the Earth plane as interference could affect the path that we are all on. Is there a point where this world may be at a point of no return, where the higher vibrations may have to act and send someone to alter the path that we are all on? Are the higher vibrations about to send a butterfly back to us to ensure things in our world recover to the way they should be?"

V: "Spirit constantly places strategic people on the Earth plane – highly evolved souls that have contracted to return and offer guidance as a physical being. We intervene and we endeavour to guide and prompt, but ultimately humankind will make their own decisions. However, as in the past, the planet has come to the point of near extinction on many occasions. There will always be a way out. We cannot say the same for humankind because as you know, over thousands of centuries, whole continents of humankind have disappeared, for whatever reason. It is very much in the power of the human spirits – spirits within the human bodies on the Earth plane. You are on pre-destined contracts, so you all actually already know that where you presently are is exactly where you are meant to be. This must be extremely difficult to comprehend as it makes you feel that you have no control over your life. But you do. As evolved souls, why would you fear dying? There is only one thing I can ever guarantee you and that is that you will come home at some point and so will your family – you will all return from the Earth plane. If you can get your head around this whilst in the physical then it will make your life a lot easier. Don't know if that helps?"

C: "It does. Thank you for those wise words."

V: "Fear not as you will all come home. This is actually just a staging post and it's not always the easiest being here on the Earth plane."

C: "Thank you for coming forward, friend."

V: "Thank you for creating the space for us to come forward. Without you we cannot come through and it is a great privilege for us to be able to do so. We send out love and light to all in this room. Peace, love and always trust. We wish you well."

C: "Thank you. Until next time."

Summary July 2023

The group's meditation this month centred on a hidden dragon that rose from the flames of hell and brought life back to a slumbering world.

Jules said that the awakening of the slumbering dragon should not necessarily indicate that mass destruction was coming to our world through intense outbreaks of fire. Jules referred to fire as cleansing tool that had the impact of regenerating our lives just as any movement of energy has the potential to bring light to our darkness.

Gordon answered the question of where this group would progress to after the final session in December 2023. Gordon said that it would not be the end of our work with the spirit team, but perhaps it was time for a new direction and new tutors to come forth. This question was asked because I was informed at the beginning of the year that our trance group would end after this experiment. This decision was made by my team of trance guides and fully accepted by myself.

Jules kindly gave us a brief biography of his time on Earth and the passion that drove his work with spirit in this dimension and the one that he currently finds himself in. He stated that he was an alchemist on the Earth plane and enjoyed many experiments involving gravity.

At the time, the group chose not to ask if this guide was in fact the famous writer Jules Verne. Individuals who were famous in their time on the Earth plane don't tend to work with my trance team, and in any case, fame and ego do not exist in the spirit dimension so the importance of this guide's identity isn't normally of any relevance.

However, it is worth noting that the spirit team agreed for this spirit person to come forward and identify as Jules. Furthermore, we were furnished with a detailed biography of the guide which suggested that his identity was of some importance to the information coming forward.

Jules also spoke about super-humans in our world that had the brain capacity to invent or discover things that made our lives better – rather like an alchemist would. He may have been hinting that such human beings are currently present in our society and ready in waiting to enhance our lives even more.

I know that I previously said that I wouldn't personally pass judgement or opinion on any of the information brought forward by the guides, but I do have to say that in almost twenty years of intensively working with trance mediums and guides that the session with Jules was the most invigorating and stimulating experience of my career to date.

We were now over halfway through this experiment and it had suddenly reached a new level. Not only that, but Jules had also inadvertently given us the title of our forthcoming book – we all agreed that 'Awakening the Slumbering Dragon' was a more appropriate title.

AUGUST 2023

*The following transcripts were obtained on Thursday 17ᵗʰ August at The Stars from Above Sanctuary, Prestwick, Ayrshire, Scotland. Eight sitters, one co-ordinator, two trance mediums (**J & A**) and two trance guides (**JOHN & CHRIS**) were involved in this session. John was the first guide to come forward.*

C o-ordinator (C): "Good evening friend, how are you this evening?"

John (J): "I am good, thank you."

C: "Who would like to ask the first question?"

Sitter 1 (S1): "Can I ask what the current state of affairs is in this world in regard to environmental changes?"

V: "There are many things happening just now within the Universe which many of you are starting to see on the television in regard to environmental issues. This will be explained further along within the next period of time for the book."

C: "Thank you friend. Can I ask who comes forward from the spirit world so that I can address the identity in the book?"

V: "John."

C: "Thank you John. Anybody else have a question for John?"

Sitter 1 (S1): "Can I ask you please, you were talking about the environment – can you see another pandemic in the near future?"

V: "What will be... will be. All I can say is that there will be more concerns over environmental issues as opposed to another pandemic, especially things happening in the climates and the oceans."

S1: "Thank you."

C: "Next question please."

Sitter 2 (S2): We spoke earlier about some of us experiencing a shift in energy fields. Some experiences have been on a personal level, but others on a higher level too. Could you explain why this is happening please?"

V: "This again is to do with the shifts in the axis of the Earth. Each individual medium feels the difference in the energies but no two people experience the same. Many will struggle and be restless through emotional turmoil and sleepless nights. Others will be more intense with greater pains and many other issues. I hope this answers your question?"

S2: "Yes thanks."

C: "John, the group discussed loops and quantum energy fields before we began this session, and we know the medium that you blend with has been advised by spirit to read a book about quantum energy. So, my question is, how important is this loop within a physical timeframe?"

V: "The loop is very important. This has been discussed before in regard to the fold in space. In particular, the hertz and the inverse hertz of the different ratios for the differing zones in time. Where we are based just now, you are sitting at zero – where travel will be minimal, whether forward or backwards within the loop. We rely on the energies of the Universe, not just your world, but the entire Universe, to be as one. Many people on Earth have different theories of relativity, but where we are there is only one. I hope that answers your query?"

C: "Yes it does, absolutely."

C: "Anybody else have a question for John?"

Sitter 3 (S3): "When the solar flares arrive on Earth, will that have major changes for our planet and for its people?"

V: "Like everything within the source of energies, solar flares will affect us and our environment, but this will realistically only affect a percentage of the population. Each individual has different aspects of different energies and this in turn affects other people's energy. So, on one hand some people will be more affected by the rise and fall of the oceans, whilst other people will be more afflicted by the effects of solar flares; shooting stars; the movement of the moon; solar eclipses, and even the subtle movements of the Earth's axis point."

C: "If we are working in a Universal loop, would I be correct in saying that the present energies in this planet could adversely affect solar flares, which in turn would fall back on us, thus creating a constant negative flow?"

V: "Yes."

C: "So, the only way to contain this would be to reverse the effects of it?"

V: "In a way, yes."

C: "And to reverse the effects of it, presumably this would require the energy fields of this planet's population to become far more positive, or more balanced?"

V: "More balanced, yes. Right now, the energies within your planet are spiking very close to a negative ratio that has only ever occurred twice before since the birth of your planet."

C: "Thank you friend. We thank you for coming forward to answer our questions and we ask that you stay close by for the remainder of the evening. We ask that you help the medium to relax as we are aware that he is struggling a bit with the connection."

C: "Thank you for coming forward. May we ask some questions?"

Chris (A): "Yes."

C: "Thank you. Can I have a question from someone please?"

Sitter 4 (S4): "Could you give us an insight into how you impact upon the medium when you are working through them so that we can understand as mediums what's going on when we work together?"

V: "The impact upon the medium really depends on the blending of the energies. If the medium can't put their own thoughts to one side, then the more resistance there is and the less clear everything becomes."

S4: "Thank you. That makes sense."

C: "Friend, you were communicating recently through the medium and you were talking about the medium's recent meditation. In particular, you were talking about the energy that was felt during the meditation. Can you elaborate more on this please?"

V: "First of all, you have to ask if it was myself communicating through the medium or was it just the medium's interpretation of the meditation. There is a struggle within each life, even though it may not be apparent to you all if what you bring forth is baggage or previous experiences. We prefer to look at you as an instrument to us and we look at how this instrument is receiving information. There needs to be a balance, and though it would always be nice to see life through eyes of positivity – where thoughts are always positive with no need to experience any negative thoughts, everybody needs to wear their own shoes and have their own experiences and you need to be mindful that not all of these experiences are easily remembered. When these particular experiences resonate in a certain way, then that would cause what we would term a resistance. I hope that makes sense?"

C: "It does, thank you. When you spoke earlier about shoes not fitting, was this just a symbolic way of saying that we need to adjust ourselves to the energies?"

V: "When you decide to come here into the physical world, you have your own personal reason for coming here. If the reason you come here is not addressed then your shoes may become too tight and start to constrict. This usually means that this is not the time or the environment, or the set of circumstances to develop at that particular stage of your existence. Does that make sense?"

C: "Yes, I think I know what you're trying to say. Anybody else have a question for Chris?"

Sitter 5 (S5): "Everybody is talking about global warming at the moment. Is this not just another natural phenomenon that occurs every so often, rather than a man-made issue?"

V: "Nature evolves over time and certain factors need to occur to bring back balance to the Earth. Not just the weight of the Earth needs to be balanced, but also the outer weight of the Universe. Earlier, you discussed quantum energy – we also need to balance the inner and outer quantum energies."

S5: "Thank you."

Sitter 6 (S6): "Can I ask please, with so much of our physical world being turned into a concrete jungle, is the forthcoming natural afflictions on our planet simply a way of the Earth claiming back it's green spaces?"

V: "The Earth doesn't hold a grudge. What you are suggesting would result in a fight that humanity would never win. The development and the progress of our planet is often tinged by greed with impure intentions, and it's here where the balance is affected. However, the Earth will always take care of itself. It's not possible for any human to change this. The structural dynamics can be shifted but the Earth will be here long after humanity."

C: "That's good to hear. We have no further questions at this time. Thank you for coming forward and giving us your insight. We understand that we often struggle with change as we are human after all. We do hope that you forgive us for all our worries but it's a human fault that we possess and will probably never end. But that's why we are here – to learn from yourselves in how to view life differently. So, please take our thanks for coming forward and we ask that you continue to work with us and give us a more balanced view on life. Many thanks."

Summary – August 2023

John came forward to say that it is unlikely that another pandemic will affect the world in the foreseeable future, however environmental issues will be a major concern.

Chris gave us an interesting analogy of the pressure placed upon our planet, stating that the weight of the Earth needs to be balanced with the outer weight of the Universe. This would suggest that perpetual balance is affected by many energy forces and the idea of a perfect world is some way far off. Furthermore, each and every individual, or every little butterfly for that matter, can affect this balance in some way or form, thus creating a constantly moving Universal continuum.

SEPTEMBER 2023

*The following transcripts were obtained on Thursday 28th September at The Stars from Above Sanctuary, Prestwick, Ayrshire, Scotland. Nine sitters, one co-ordinator, two trance mediums (**K** & **M**) and two trance guides (**UNNAMED** & **GORDON**) were involved in this session. The first guide to come forward didn't give us a name as their identity was deemed unimportant.*

Co-ordinator (C): "Welcome friend, thank you for coming forward this evening."

Unnamed (K): "It is so good to be here amongst you in this form. Indeed, it is a pleasure to be here with you all."

C: "It is a great pleasure for all of us as well."

V: "I wish to give a short explanation in relation to the change in the energy in this vibration and I hope it will become a bit clearer. There are many different forms of vibrational energy at work in the spirit world and right now a different form of energy is requiring a bit more of a blend with this group. This takes a more focussed approach from the group and requires you not to waver too much and remain focussed to the energy right in front of you. It is very important that you do not break this focus as it will allow us to work in a deeper level with you. Are you all okay with this?"

C: "Yes we are, thank you."

V: "You may think that you sit there without working, but you are as each one of you has a unique energy field around you and without your energy then this communication could not take place – it would be impossible. There must always be a control and there must always be a focus. The collective energies of the group must have intentions that are pure and of truth – as you all are. That is why we bring this new energy to you this evening. We hope that you enjoy it as we are certainly glad to be here amongst you all too."

C: "Thank you friend. May we ask that you give us a name so that we may identify you in respect of the recording and future written publication?"

V: "No names. There is no need for names as you must understand that we come here on a different vibration and we are beyond using names. It is very much a privilege for us to be here, but we do not have any need for a name, simply because our vibration has reached a different level where we have no need for a name. If we were to pluck a name from somewhere it would just be something simple, so we do not mind if you want to pick something. It is not important to us to be truthful; we are just glad to be here communicating with you on this level; at this time; in this *now* moment. As was said earlier – it is a *now* moment. We will not dilute the energy with any trivialities if you don't mind."

C: "Yes, we totally understand and we are quite happy with communicating on a nameless format."

V: "You have all reached a level where you can work here in a comfortable way and are able to blend your energies in a way that complements this newer energy. There are some who would question this energy and there are some who would be afraid of this energy, but we would encourage you to embrace this energy. You are now part of this energy and it cannot exist without you. You are creators; you are producers; you are part of this energy – it is a product of your work. Do you understand this?"

C: "Yes."

V: "It is most important that you continue to work in this field as it is part of *your* progress in *your* evolution of *your* spirit. You can, of course, ask any questions if you wish, but you must be aware that we may not answer to your specification. But you already know that. Please proceed."

C: "Thank you. Would anyone like to ask the first question?"

Sitter 1 (S1): "There are many concerns on the Earth plane at this specific time and we are all trying to remain positive. Is there anything that you can add that would assist us in retaining a positive attitude?"

V: "You are correct that you must retain a positive attitude in the face of any chaos that may come your way. We will always remind you that you are a very steadying force for those around you and this is very important. Your purpose here; and your aim on the Earth plane; is to bring a sense of peace to those around you, rather than be sucked into the collective consciousness that strives to maintain chaos. It is your objective to be part of the collective unconsciousness that strives for peace and harmony in a co-existence. We know that you are aware of the importance of the Earth and our connection to the Earth. We are part of the Earth, as it is part of us. We are very much involved in the creation of the people who are sent to the Earth in order to aid it. We can only hope that they succeed in their mission as we cannot directly interfere in their mission – we can only guide or help where we can as interference is something that we cannot do. So, you are here on the Earth, you are living the Earthly existence and you must rise to the challenge. When I say rise to the challenge, I do not mean that you must fight or take up arms with anyone – that is not the challenge. The challenge is simply one of peace – it always has been and it always will be. So, the challenge for you, my friends, is to retain peace."

S1: "Thank you."

C: "Anybody else have a question to ask?"

Sitter 2 (S2): "In my earlier meditation, there was a bit of chaos in my visualisation, almost as if I was watching it through a window. How do you retain a peaceful mind when this is going on around you and you have a sense that you cannot stop this chaos? Also, does this mean that some of us will have to physically remove ourselves from this predicament?"

V: "You are not an observer in your own life – you are a co-creator in your own life and a co-dependant in your own life. You must act as you can destroy chaos in only a moment. You have the ability to deal with this as you are the most important being in amongst your own chaos. The reality is that you have indeed contributed to the chaos, suffice to say that you can end it or you can step back from it. But you definitely don't need to be involved in it. Does that help?"

S2: "Kind of."

V: "Well, you may ask another question and we will try to clear that up for you."

S2: "I just had a sense that where I was in the meditation didn't feel safe and I've never experienced that feeling before. I felt that my only way forward was to remove myself from the situation and face the problem from the outside rather than being stuck with this surrounding me."

V: "I understand where you are coming from. You are always safe and you are well protected. However, if you feel that you are in any physical danger then of course you must remove yourself from this place in your physical world. Spiritually, you are a higher evolved being and you are able to change things around you or you are able to change yourself, by that, I mean that you cannot be driven by your emotions as you can rise above them. I will now contradict myself by saying this, but you can observe the chaos without being part of it. Unless you wish to be part of it. Believe it or not, some people do wish to be part of the chaos, but you, my child, are safe – you always have been and you will continue to be. Helpful?"

S2: "Yes, thank you."

V: "There is a question here; I feel needs to be asked?"

C: "Yes, but I'm a little apprehensive to ask it."

V: "Don't worry; it is just my energy that is in a different vibration and sometimes because I am far removed from the human being that I previously was, I often come across as a bit matter of fact."

C: "Forgive me but it is not the energy that is making me apprehensive, but the question itself."

V: "That is okay because I may not be able to answer it for many reasons."

C: "Okay thanks. My question is regarding the highest energies from the next dimension. They do not appear to have any emotions. Is this because they have learned to exist without emotions or did they never possess any emotions in the first place?"

V: "Emotions are a very important part of the human existence and the human existence is a very important part of the spiritual being, so emotions are naturally tied to the spiritual being. It is not that we have evolved from emotions so that we do not feel them anymore, because we do. Believe it or not, when you listen to me it may not sound like it, but we have so much love for each and every one of you. We are all tied together in the pursuit of peace, love, and harmony. So, there are emotions, but not in the same way as you experience them here in the physical, human existence. The human existence is awash with emotions and all that we ask is that you acknowledge these emotions as it is part of your experience here. In fact, for the most part, it is why you chose to be in a human existence. However, you are not that emotion; you are the spiritual being living a human existence, but not the actual emotion itself. You are not fear as you rise above fear. You are not pity as you rise above being pitied. And if you should feel enlightened, then you should enlighten others. It won't be the emotion that achieves this; it will be your spirit. Does that answer your question?"

C: "Yes, wise words, many thanks. Does anyone want to ask another question?"

Sitter 3 (S3): "Can I ask about various dreams I have been having in regard to rebirth. In particular I have been seeing the sea on fire. Does this dream signify rebirth or is there another more sinister meaning?"

V: "Perhaps this dream signifies a worry that you have in regard to fuel – gas or oil. Perhaps you have been reading about problems with this form of energy in your world. Or perhaps this is something that is continually in your mind for another reason. We will say, and we have said it before, that fire is cleansing – as is water. What you may be seeing in your vision is simply a method of cleansing. Perhaps, in a sense, cleansing your own energy and energies all around you. Does this help?"

S3: "Yes, could that also mean that the Earth is being cleansed?"

V: "The Earth is continually being cleansed. We continually give the Earth a vibrational energy. The Earth gives so much to us and we are continually helping the Earth by sending beings to help it. The Earth is such a precious being and you should continue to send your healing energy and your cleansing energy to sustain it."

S3: "Thank you."

V: "It is time for me to take a step back but I am happy to take one more question?"

Sitter 4 (S4): "If I could quickly ask about my personal meditation tonight. I found myself under the ocean and I had a feeling that there was a crack in the ocean and it was allowing spiritual knowledge to be released. Does this make sense to you?"

V: "The ocean is a being unto itself and as you all live quite close to the sea, you will often see the different moods of the ocean. The ocean is very nurturing with many different life forms. You are also tied to the ocean as your human body is made up of water. The Earth has many oceans, rivers, and streams and in many ways is tied to your spiritual journey, so spiritual knowledge may be obtained from what lies beneath every ocean. Does that help?"

S4: "Yes thank you for that analogy."

V: "I believe you have another question?"

S4: "Yes, I was also feeling a different vibration during the meditation."

V: "Indeed you were."

S4: "Yes, it felt like my hands were on train tracks – as if a powerful energy was vibrating through me."

V: "We are connecting with you on a higher level and it is up to you whether you allow this higher energy to keep working with you. All I will say is that you are ready for this."

S4: "Thank you."

C: "Friend, may I ask a final question?

V: "You may."

C: "We are all very much aware of incoming conflict in our physical world. We know it's coming but we do not know at what level or capacity. Can I ask, when this conflict is over, will we need to rebuild the Earth physically and spiritually?"

V: "The Earth is in a state of constant flux. There is always something breaking down and being renewed in the Earth. This is the way of the being that is the Earth – it is always in a state of rebirth. And it always will be. Things break down; they compost and then subsequently feed the Earth, allowing things to grow. That is the way of the Earth. We do not interfere with that."

C: "I understand. Thank you for coming forward. It has been an absolute pleasure for us to be in the company of such wisdom and knowledge."

V: "I thank you for allowing me to work with you all. I understand that I can come across as somewhat imposing. That is not my intention. My intention is to help your spiritual trance journey and I hope that has been achieved this evening."

C: "It has, very much so, thank you."

V: "I bid you all a very good evening.

Co-ordinator I: "Thank you for coming forward, Gordon. I feel that you have some important information for us."

Gordon (M): "There is an urgency here as in order to manage the quest there needs to be a real focus on these final sessions. Does anyone need to ask anything?"

C: "Yes please. We need help to get this message out – you know that and we know that. Are you working with other groups or individual mediums throughout the world; sharing the same message, so that we can help each other to make reason to everything that has been stated so far?"

V: "As my esteemed colleague said earlier, we have placed individuals in your world with special skills, albeit with some aspects of learning still to be attained. These people are all over the physical world. There are also people in powerful positions who have great influence over your world – but they could be considered good or bad, depending on how you look at things. You must remember that without good you would not be able to see evil and vice-versa. So, the answer to your question is that there are many individuals in the physical world who have great influence within themselves to make changes to your world, but your interpretation of their actions may differ."

"I know that there is a lot of anxiety amongst people about what might happen, but you must remember that you could all return home by tomorrow. So, why worry about it – worry won't change anything apart from the atmosphere that you are living in. And worry creates fear. And fear is the biggest concern. Fear is much more than a word. Once it sneaks into your subconscious then you struggle to sleep and start to worry even more. You worry about your children or elderly parents but the reality is that you can't change what is still to happen. The answer is to find a moment and send peace and love to anyone who is feeling this way – that's all you can ever really do. Does this make sense?"

C: "Yes it does. Thank you, Gordon."

V: "When you come back home, and as your spirit evolves, your soul will bring all the information back. It's only then that you will have to think about your next journey. Just like the journey here that you all decided to take. You're not here by chance. You're here because you decided to come here. However, you didn't come here because there is going to be something happening in the physical world for the very first time, because everything that happens in the future has already happened in the past."

Sitter 5 (S5): "Can I ask you a question, Gordon? I have been experiencing a sense that whatever is coming is an accumulation of everything malevolent that has happened in the past. For example, lessons not learned from, in respect of chaotic instances that have blighted our past. To me, this felt like a way of cleansing, and I saw this as a little butterfly flew past. Would this be a true reflection of what we are about to experience?"

V: "If these experiences didn't happen then you would not have the experience to learn from them. You see, it's not change that's the concern here – it's the fear of change. It's how you respond or react when change seems drastic. You must remember that not everyone is evolved to the same point as yourselves. There is a cycle, a loop, circles upon circles, it's part of the whole process. I don't know if that analogy has answered your question or not?"

S5: "People have commented on world wars every 100 years or so and I just feel that what is coming is a mixture of all that has gone on before."

V: "My observation is that the world, and the way that the world functions in regard to humans, has changed so much. The first two World Wars were not fought through the means of the media and much of what took place was hidden from the masses. Whereas any future conflict would become graphically available in an instant to almost anyone who wished to view it. The main problem here is that constant negativity will bombard our world and create great challenges for our emotional well-being. There will inevitably be no escape from it and everyone will ultimately feel a part of it. How you deal with this will determine how you evolve as a spirit. We will never directly interfere in any conflict but we will always send messages to anyone who desires them. You must continue to meditate and be content within your own existence on this planet. The one thing you can do is be kind, loving, caring, and remain non-judgemental. But also remember that you are still here to learn lessons, so you might not always be as loving as you can be. This is just part of the life cycle, and also part of your journey. Does that help?"

S5: "Yes, very much so."

V: "Before I go, I would like you all to applaud your-selves. Remember, without you, we would not be able to communicate our thoughts and advice. Thank you."

C: "Thank you Gordon."

Summary – September 2023

A trance guide came forward during this session declaring that a new energy vibration was now working with the group and extra focus would be needed to blend with this energy. This guide preferred to remain unnamed as they were beyond names in their vibration.

The main message being given by this guide is that our mission is not to warn the world about upcoming conflict or terrify an unsuspecting public that seems oblivious to the impending energy change. It is simply to bring peace and understanding to everyone we meet, regardless of their views or prejudices.

This powerful message reinforced the group's willingness to keep going with our monthly sessions. There is no doubt that the information previously brought forward had begun to affect our thoughts every night as we went to sleep. The group discussed beforehand how our dreams were becoming more and more synonymous with our perceptions and challenges of the forthcoming future. It was also becoming more and more difficult not to discuss what had been digested in these sessions with our friends and family. Now we were beginning to understand just exactly why we were here in this place at this precise moment in time. The importance of this experiment was beginning to hit home.

Gordon stated that he knew that there was a great deal of anxiety and fear within this group and understood why that would be the case. He reiterated that we are all capable of dealing with these emotions and that we are where we are right now because we have been placed here by the spirit team.

Gordon said that it wasn't 'change' that was our major concern, but the fear of change. Gordon also said that 'change' happens so that you have the opportunity to learn from it.

Gordon highlighted the fact that when our world moves into the next stage of 'change' then it will become graphically available to everyone in an instant. It will be how we react emotionally to this 'change' that will determine our next step along the path to spiritual advancement.

OCTOBER 2023

*The following transcripts were obtained on Thursday 19th October at The Stars from Above Sanctuary, Prestwick, Ayrshire, Scotland. Nine sitters, one co-ordinator, one trance medium (**S**) and one trance guide (**Unnamed**) were involved in this session. The trance guide asked to remain anonymous. It became clear during the session that the trance guide was a highly evolved spirit that has worked with us many times before.*

C o-ordinator (C): "Welcome friend, thank you for coming forward this evening to communicate with us. Do you wish to address the group before we begin with questions?"

Unnamed (S): "We have been watching what you have been doing this evening and the format is perfect. This is a good thing, is it not?"

C: "Yes."

V: "This is what your planet is all about – experimenting and you have been doing exactly that, this evening."

C: "Thank you."

V: "We are not here to give you answers to what is happening on your planet. We have come to you because you called us and we are here as a support to you all, but not to give you the answers to your issues."

C: "We appreciate that."

V: "We do not need to tell you what will happen in a day or a week, or even a month or a year. It is already playing out. The fear is great again, but do you not understand that this scenario has already played out before, and who knows may play out again. Your planet is a planet of vast experience. Do you realise how many souls are waiting to incarnate? Yes, there seems to be suffering and there are horrendous things happening, but to balance this, your planet is moving and shifting into a different reality. What you are witnessing just now is simply souls incarnating to learn lessons from previous incarnations. You look at the baby who is born only for a short time, or the teenager kidnapped, or the grandmother murdered. I think this resonates with you. Have you not experienced that before? We are here to give you tools to navigate your way through what is happening. We have given you these tools before. You connect to your planet; you remain grounded, and you eat well."

C: "Thank you."

V: "Since the last conflict, look at how much technology has advanced in your planet. In the past, you would have not known what was happening all over your planet. Yet, the same atrocities were taking place. Now, you will instantly know every time conflict occurs and this will impact your lives in a much greater scale – if you choose to let it."

C: "Thank you friend. Can I ask you where you are from and if there is an identity that you wish to give us?"

V: "We have decided that this is just a communication so that you are given things to navigate. There are many friends in the background who will answer your questions. Is this okay with you?"

C: "We understand this, thank you, and we appreciate the information is more important than the name of the communicator."

V: "When you talk about light-workers, do you know what this means? It simply means that you work with the light. You don't look externally to see the light as to be a light-worker you only work internally. Presently, the majority of people are looking externally for help and light-workers are there to shine their light through their heart - shine unconditional love and passion to all."

C: "If the people won't listen to us when we pass on your information to them, then what can we do to convince them of this?"

V: "The more that you work internally, and the more work that you do on yourself, the more you will be able to express your feelings and experiences to others. You must expand your heart so that it sends unconditional love in the way of others. They will then pick up on that vibration and they will be drawn towards you."

C: "I understand, so presumably the meditation that we had tonight was to clear our minds from the angry mob. Is this important that we cleanse our own soul before we can teach others?"

V: "Absolutely. These unpleasant feelings that you experience when you watch your media sources can be addressed if you go internally and simply dissolve all negative feelings. If you feel hurt – is that not an indication that your soul is giving you the opportunity to cleanse and move forward? I would think so."

C: "What would we do if our families in the physical world are affected directly by violence in the forthcoming conflict?"

V: "Again, you simply must go internal to the innermost parts of your soul; sit on a bench and meditate – that is what you are here for. Pass unconditional love to others and they will pick up on this vibration. You will have the knowledge and the tools to achieve this. We will give you the tools which you can then pass on to others. The fear is great, of course, but you must remain grounded and aware of your full physical capacity. All we ask is that you project the light. What you are witnessing is a reality chosen by others. What you must now do is simply choose your own reality by passing love and compassion. Before you can do this, you must be aware of your part in this great time – this Great Awakening."

C: "Thank you friend. I know you said that you were not here to take questions, but I do believe that one of the sitters has a very important question to ask. Would it be okay for this question to be asked?"

V: "Yes, of course."

C: "Who has the question? Remember, you won't know unless you ask it."

V: "If nobody wants to ask the question, then I will endeavour to answer it. I can show you an alternative way of projecting love and remaining non-judgemental. There will be great judgemental energy around your planet and fear amongst humans will greatly increase. However, look at the beggar on the street and think of how many people passing by who would pass judgement on the plight of this individual. Wouldn't the purpose of the beggar being there at that precise time have a huge effect on the personal journey of everyone else, rather than the beggar themselves? Would you not say that the beggar is in fact projecting love and compassion to an unsuspecting mass of individuals? All we are asking is that you honour your Buddha; your light within yourself and also within others – without judgement. Even a young child will pick up on your vibration. Do you not think that when a child sits on your knee as you offer comfort and support, that it is in fact the child that is comforting you? Remember a young child will not have had to deal with judgemental energy in the way that you almost certainly have. A child will not have had to experience the issues relating to religion, politics, or evil deeds. So, we ask that you go back to how you felt as a child with unconditional love in your heart towards yourself and towards others."

C: "Thank you."

V: "We are really pleased and grateful for the group you have assembled here. You meet regularly and you work on yourselves, and this makes our job much easier to connect and support you. Not simply to give you answers, but to support you and give you tools, especially at this time of unsettledness. You must trust that all is where it should be and that you are in a position of being fully awake and ascending, you must understand this. Keep your energy high and be the light workers that you are, in order to project the love to others in this stressful time for many."

C: "Thank you friend for those wise words."

V: "I thank you for allowing me to speak. There are friends who will come forward and answer more questions. We ask that you take a few of your minutes and go inside to think of questions that aren't about your world's atrocities, rather think of things that might help you walk your path without fear. You are only human after all, fear will still surface, but this is okay. You are here to once again experience what has transpired before. Remember to say 'I am...', because I am."

C: "Thank you. We apologise that you didn't get the question but we do thank you for answering it anyway, as I know that you possess the ability to do this. Thank you for also working with a fellow medium – it was nice to hear your voice once again. Go with our love. Namaste."

Summary – October 2023

Before our meeting in October, I was informed by my spirit team that one of the sitters in the group would be a guest trance medium for the night and that they were busy organising this behind the scenes. Sure enough, the trance medium that was scheduled for October telephoned to say that he was unwell and couldn't attend. Therefore, the guest trance medium was asked to step in and obligingly did so. It then became apparent to me during the session that the guide coming forward was Mr Chung from my spirit team, which was an absolute delight for me personally, although the guide did state that an identity was not necessary in this communication.

The spirit team had also informed me beforehand that they had organised a particular style of meditation to be used prior to this session beginning. This involved the group being able to find a quiet spot in their mind whilst listening to the recording of a street riot being played out. The objective here was clearly to see how we would react to the chaos all around us. I watched the group enter a deep hypnotic state almost instantly and was impressed that none of them were affected by the chaotic sounds that filled the room. This test had been passed with flying colours.

The guide said that our planet was moving and shifting into a different reality, yet he said that we have all been here before. He also said that we are all here to learn from previous incarnations. Does this indicate that we have all been involved in a previous world conflict?

The guide stated that what we are about to experience is a reality chosen by others, so we must choose a different reality that involves finding our innermost peace regardless of the surroundings. In essence, the meditation we had just enjoyed enhanced the fact that this is possible if you can just find the knowhow.

In my experience, this guide has always possessed the ability to read the minds of those in our trance circle and would often answer a question before it had even been asked. In this session, one of the sitters had a question but was reluctant to ask it and the guide knew this – hence he answered it with his usual aplomb. This was most pleasing for me to witness it happening through another trance medium. Ironically, this was the first time that this spirit guide would publicly admit that conflict in our world was inevitable, which is a sobering thought considering I have never personally known him to bring forward information that never came to fruition.

The guide stated that we should all remember that the beggar on the street is of no more or less importance than the decision-makers in our society. Therefore, we should treat everyone with respect as we move to this new reality.

NOVEMBER 2023

*The following transcripts were obtained on Thursday 23rd November at The Stars from Above Sanctuary, Prestwick, Ayrshire, Scotland. Four sitters, one co-ordinator, three trance mediums (**K, M & A**) and three trance guides (**Oephilia, CHRIS & The Blossom**) were involved in this session.*

Co-ordinator (C): "Welcome friend."

Oephilia (M): "I am honoured to be here this evening. There is much to be said."

C: "Thank you for coming forward."

V: "I thank you for the energy that you are all sending and it is essential that you continue to keep sending this energy to us this evening as there is much information to come through. You have all gained the perception of the reality of your many lives, which, in the scheme of things, are but pebbles dropped in the sea. This life is a fleeting life, and when you are living in it, it feels so intense with all the feelings in your physical body. The key is the spirit and this is essentially part that needs to be nurtured, cherished, and maintained. Unfortunately, we live in a world where many people have got side-tracked and they do not maintain the same level of care and consideration to the spirit."

"So, I say to you, each day thank your spirit and do not forget it is there and essentially it is the part of you that is eternal and returns to the supreme power. So always, always, be aware of that. That is why when you go into your meditations you will realise how insignificant a lot of what happens on physical planets is – it is only there so that the spirit can learn and bring back information that's then shared with the source. The source then expands and as it expands the light spreads. All that we are requiring from you is your light, your healing, and your love. When that is out there in the world – then the world is happy, the world is joyful and all things are as they should be."

"When you look back in time, yes things were simpler, but that is not to say that all the new technology has created problems – it has simply created more lessons for souls to develop. And remember that not all souls are at the same spiritual level as it depends on how many lifetimes you have had, how many experiences or how many opportunities you have had. But not just that, it's what you've learned. You hear people saying, 'I'm the oldest, so I know the most.' It's not what you know but what you've learnt, and that is what it's all about."

"The world is also learning through all these difficult times that we are all facing and this is as it should be. It is the physical experiences that make people anxious and fearful. Spiritual beings that are mature realise that this current situation is part of our learning curve and it is imperative that we exist in the moment. Rushed energy creates anxiety so we must stay in the moment so that the spirit and the body stay as one – that is all anyone ever has to work on."

"I hope that this has been of interest to you as it is key to your development. I am going to withdraw now because there is much more information to come forward this evening. I thank you for this opportunity to communicate again."

C: "Thank you friend for those wise words. Do you wish to give us your name for the purposes of the publication?"

V: "You can give me any name you wish as it is irrelevant."

C: "Thank you my friend."

V: "Can I just finish by saying that there are many of us in this room and we are all watching, listening, and learning. That is primarily why we are here – to learn from you. We are as one."

C: "Thank you."

C: "Good evening."

CHRIS (A): "Good evening."

C: "Thank you for coming forward, friend. You have been listening to all that has been spoken about this evening and hopefully you've heard some wise words. We would just like to ask if you would like to contribute further to what has already been said, or in a way, summarise from all that has been discussed before?"

V: "Going forward, people talk about the Great Awakening. The awakening essentially is, in human form, taking back your own power, rather than being drawn into what is being played out in front of you. You come to realise that there are certain possibilities in life that you might not necessarily understand. You have to go within and work with meditations – that's your training ground. It's not all about what others would have you believe as what plays out directly in front of you is never that important. The bigger picture will show you these infinite possibilities. Your perception and your perspective all changes within this energy that we share. The vibration within this shared energy is what connects us and it is here that we finally become as one."

"Everything within life is just a vibration. Raise your vibration and join in as this is essentially all you need to do. Remember all you need to do is feel love and just be you."

C: "Thank you friend for your wise words."

V: "Thank you."

C: "Do you wish to give us a name for the publication?"

V: "Any name of your choice."

C: "Thank you, friend."

C: "We are aware of your presence, friend."

The Blossom (K): "Good evening, all."

C: "Good evening to you. Thank you for coming forward and gracing us with your presence."

V: "You are most welcome. It is my pleasure to be here in your group"

C: "Thank you."

V: "I would also like to say that it is our group, for we are as one together."

C: "Thank you."

V: "As our energies blend and merge, and as we settle into this energy here, can you now feel these energies blend in this room?"

C: "Yes we can."

V: "We thank you for bringing this energy with you. It is very much appreciated what you bring here. There are many thoughts going round in your heads, and there are many things that you question since they perturb you. And we would just like to speak a little on these particular things. What a wonderful meditation you had this evening – you visited your past, your future, and of course your present moment in time. They are all linked but they are just part of a cycle, or a loop – for you are all in a loop. At this moment in time, it is very important to you to focus on this loop, for it is in this loop that you are working on your spiritual being, your awakening and on yourself. This loop will take you back to where you came from and you will have your experiences here, further adding them to many other experiences and many other loops."

"We would like to say that the path that you visited is just part of you, and you may have visited some trauma. When you experience this trauma, you must understand that it is no longer in existence – it is merely a stepping stone to a transition of your future self. In your future self you will see the evolution of your growth and your soul evolvement, and this is what you came back for."

"We love that you are so tied to the Earth as we have much respect for this Earth. It is such a wonderful being for you to be part of and there are many things to be learned here. You will learn to see yourself as we see you, for you are a spiritual being. We, in the spiritual realms, have designed the human body to mirror the spiritual body too. Of course, we have to put you into a small frame, unlike when you are free flowing as a beam of light. In this human body, you are not simply a visitor to the human body – you are a co-creator of the human body. You designed it to house your spiritual self and you are a co-dependant as you need the body to have your experiences on the Earth plane. You must ensure that you are thankful to the Earth for your time spent here as the Earth allows you to be here. We give to the Earth and the Earth gives to us. We are very much co-dependants to the Earth and also co-creators, but you create your own environment. You are very much motivated by your growth and by your evolution – which is also tied to the many cycles of the Earth. If you live your best life here then naturally this will lift your spirit and it will add to the many, many experiences that you have had in the past."

"The past, as I previously said, is a stepping stone to the future, and the future is just a part of what you are now and what you shall become. You have already lived that future; you have already become that being; you are that being – that very essence of yourself. It is in this process of evolving that you then become all-knowing and at one with the source of universal love and light. For you are part of it; you do not strive to be it, you simply are it. You are the 'I am'. You always have been, it's just that you have learned to wake up a little more."

"Those who sit in this room are much awakened. Your vibrational energy is very, very good. However, you must live a whole life as that is why you are here. You are here to experience everything, because as spiritual beings we do not have the sense of smell or taste, but when you are here on the Earth plane then you must experience these things. You must take joy in them and you must take joy in the vibration of the Earth. You must also live in harmony with those around you. You are not a single entity – you are part of so much more. You are part of the Universe of light and the Universe of love. It is a part of you and you are a part of it. You are at one and you must fulfil what you came here for."

"What is that you ask? What is the meaning of life? Many have asked that question in the past, but what they really mean is 'what is the meaning of death?' Those who ask what the meaning of life is – actually fear death. Life is infinite; there is no death. Of course, there is death of the shell of the body. These things must die off because this is part of our contract with the Earth. The Earth evolves in a material way as well as environmentally, and this energy must be fulfilled. Part of our contract is to inhabit the shell or the body and to help with the creation and the evolution of the Earth and its entire species."

"We do not live above the Earth; we live in a parallel co-existence with the Earth. We can pop in and out of the energy here and also inhabit the human body and other forms of creatures, but we do not try to harness the forces of nature within the Earth. We do not wish to change the forces of the Earth; we simply want to co-exist with the Earth. We are co-inhabitants and we respect and cherish our time here spent on the Earth."

We, of course, wish that you are happy here as that way you will bring peace to others around you. Very few of you will live a single life so it is very important that in every aspect that you share your energy with others, showing capacity and empathy to them so that they may also find peace from within. There are people who are not quite ready for the next part of their journey yet as they are still at an infant stage of their evolution. They are not quite ready to listen to your words but do not let that deter you. There is still a part of them that is ready to be awakened, however they are not at the stage where everything you say will reverberate with them, and they will highly likely return to the Earth to begin the next part of their evolving journey."

"Those of you who sit in this room have all awakened to this vibrational energy and you are very much in touch with the spiritual realms. This can be enhanced through your meditations and your quiet times. You do not need to sit in a darkened room chanting - you can simply take a walk on the beach. Every time you sit alone you connect with your inner being, and you also connect with us. We often dip in and out of your energy and sometimes you are or aren't aware of this fact; however, we will not interfere with you. We will merely help and guide you with this process. You will never feel left alone with any doubts or fears; we will always be there to nurture you. You are not children to us – you are an equal. You are in the same footing as us. You will find that we have reversed roles in previous times – you have helped us and we have helped you. That is the way that it has been, the way it is now, and the way it always will be. We must uphold the spiritual laws. We must respect the Earth. We must respect and honour each other. That is how we awaken. Your vibration is very important and your time here is important. You must live well and enjoy it."

"I thank you for listening to these words and I hope that they have been of some help to you. But, if not, you may ask us questions in your sleep state tonight. Your spiritual helpers and guides will endeavour to answer your questions. As you know, many of the answers lie inside you. In other words, you already know the answers, but sometimes it just takes a little jolt to help you to realise your potential. I thank you for the energies tonight as they have been amazing."

C: "Thank you friend. Do you wish to give us your name for the purposes of recording these words to the book?

V: "You may call me 'The Blossom' if you wish. There are many of us here, but we realise you may like a title for your book. We have something that we all wish to say to the co-ordinator, and that is to believe in yourself as you are having a crisis of confidence at the moment. Do not worry about this as we are with you and we are always here to help you."

C: "Thank you friend for those comforting words, they are much appreciated.

Summary – November 2023

November was deemed the opportunity for the trance guides to begin a summarisation of everything that had been brought to the table.

The first trance guide was Oephilia. We were reminded that whenever we enter our meditations, we suddenly realise that any turmoil going on in the physical world seems rather insignificant. This is how events in our planet appears to those watching in the spirit dimension – almost like dropping pebbles in the sea. We were also informed that all the experiences shared in this fleeting physical lifetime are brought home to the source and used appropriately to spread the light to others. No experience is ever worthless, even if its tinged with fear, regret, and malice.

Next to come forward was CHRIS. We were then given an extremely powerful statement – 'The awakening essentially is, in human form, taking back your own power, rather than being drawn into what is being played out in front of you.' The important aspect being that we all have our own personal power and that is essentially the most important part of our journey here. This is what we will all be judged on when we return home and not what others have impressed upon us.

Then we were reminded to simply raise our vibration; feel love, and above all else… just be YOU.

The Blossom came forward and reminded us of our earlier meditation, where we were all taken on a journey to our past, future and back to our present moment. The Blossom spoke about the importance of our personal loop and how we must understand the dynamics and principles of this energy force.

The Blossom stated that you do not need to sit in darkness, chanting to your God in order to experience the ultimate meditation. You can simply go for a walk along the beach and there you just may find your inner self offering you guidance and direction when all seems lost.

The Blossom reminded us that many of the answers to the questions already lie within us.

DECEMBER 2023

The following transcripts were obtained on Thursday 7th *December at The Stars from Above Sanctuary, Prestwick, Ayrshire, Scotland. Seven sitters, one co-ordinator, one trance medium* (**D**) *and three trance guides* (**Mr Chung, ISAC &** **Gordon**) *were involved in this session.*

C o-ordinator (C): "Welcome friend, thank you for coming forward."

Chung (D): "We wish to thank each and every one of you, not only for your attendance this evening, but for your presence over the full term of this experiment. For many of your linear years now, we have been researching and organising these meetings, we hope you understand this. We have an obligation to the Earth and to the Universe to ensure that whatever affects it must also benefit it in an alternative way. With your backing and your help, we will achieve this. In your meditations you were taken home as this is your home and this is your place to be."

"When you signed your contract to return to this physical institution, your main purpose was to break free from previous memories of this world that you have been tied to. It is your primary mission and we can now inform you that you have achieved your objectives. We congratulate you all on this feat."

"Whatever is happening in the physical dimension, whether it be mass emotional fear or hateful anger that has surfaced from people stuck in their loops, this will not personally affect your own development. Your main objective was to break free from your own self-developed loop and then simply return home. You have all now achieved this freedom – congratulations! If everyone on this Earth achieved what you have all achieved then the forthcoming predicament would not take place. There would be no need for this. But, alas, there is a necessity for what is to come as conditions must be put in place to challenge those who have forgotten why they chose to visit the physical plane. For many individuals, they will almost certainly remain in their loops, returning to the spiritual plane completely unfulfilled due to not being able to adjust their thoughts in a way that atones for past demeanours. There are great opportunities for everyone on this physical plane to once again ensure that the Earth can be at peace with itself. To do this, everyone must return to a state of spiritual laws and not be obsessed by materialistic ways. Materialism is the main cause of the discontent in your world and it will inevitably create conflict between those who seek power through wealth and those who strive to avoid this. There can only ever be the one success story here – just as it has always been. However, it will take a considerable amount of your time for everyone to realise this. One moment please."

ISAC (V): "Good evening. We wish you to pass on this information to those who are not present this evening - our indebted thanks for all of their participation in this experiment. We have broken down the group into this smaller circle this evening as this is all that's necessary to achieve the final conclusion. We congratulate you on your attendance here this evening. We must apologise for extensively using your energies to fulfil our obligations, but we realise that you have given this willingly and not against your wishes. This will be our final meeting as all that has needed to be said… has been said. It is up to the people to now make their own future. You can only stand by and witness their path and their journey until it's complete. You have fulfilled your obligations and your contract has been signed and completed. You can return home when you wish."

"The greatest challenge to mankind is not death… but life… and the realisation that you cannot kill a person – only their dreams. Until this is realised, you must once again step upon this Earth and refrain from repeating past errors of judgement. Only when mankind is stripped bare of all possessions does mankind realise what's important. Love cannot be purchased or stolen. It can only be found through endless battles of desperation, defeat, fear, or broken heartedness. Love rises from our greatest low points, just as fortitude never did fear the brave."

"There will be a time when all of you here will be at the stage that I have just spoken about. You cannot escape from your empathetic ways. We will not desert you at that precise moment. We are only ever a single thought away."

"There will come a time when physical bodies cannot die and all emotions will be eradicated. At this point, you will gladly wish to return to the physical world and to carbonised bodies that are full of emotions. This may be your next adventure – just like that of my own!"

Chung (D): "What you have been listening to this evening should remain within this group. The recordings will be published and every reader will be able to interpret these words in their own way. Even though you have a grasp of this knowledge and you are beginning to understand where we come from, there will be a time not too far away when things will be a little topsy-turvy. When this occurs, your spiritual awareness will increase and your human awareness will decrease. You understand?"

C: "Yes."

V: "Ironically, in many ways we hope that you do not understand this. However, we know that you have almost certainly been in a similar situation and you have returned here in your own free will. You do not have to escape from your past. Your past is what made you what you are today. Your experiences taught you what is necessary for your future. We all wish to know what our future entails. Well, I can tell you of the incredible riches ahead for you that you will all enjoy. Richness of brotherhood; of sisterhood, of kindred spirits. What you will return to will be the ultimate dream with no regrets. Your paradise is all but a thought in your mind and I congratulate you on achieving your dream."

"This experiment has been as much a part of all of you as it has been a part of us. We all have just the one objective and that is to enlighten those who fear this inevitable conflict. The prize at the end of this conflict is worth every battle. We can assure you all of that."

ISAC (D): "It is none but the wiser or the richer. It is none but the poorer or the fool. In abundance we strive for the perfect establishment, but as individuals we often fail at the first attempt. Nevertheless, together we can achieve the improbable. When all of you here are as one with us... then we are indestructible. Be proud of yourselves. We are proud of you."

Gordon (D): "Good evening, everyone. Oh, what a wonderful energy surrounds us all tonight. On behalf of the trance medium and all the guides around us, it is a delight to be present with you all. The trance medium has given me the opportunity to simply pop in and answer a few of your personal questions. My dear, would you switch off the electronic recording device as this part shall remain private to you all as a matter of respect for everything that each and every one of you have given us over the length of this experiment. It has been a blast!"

C: "I will Gordon, thank you."

Summary — December 2023

I was instructed by my spirit team that they wished to address the group through my own trance mediumship, so that they could give a final update on everything that had been brought forward in the past year.

Chung was the first guide to come forward and he thanked the group for their dedication over the last year. Chung explained that this experiment had begun many years ago and it had taken until now to find the correct blend of energies needed to facilitate the outcome.

Chung congratulated the group on successfully identifying and breaking free from their personal loops, and for fulfilling their obligations to their contracts. Chung confirmed that all members of this group would now ascend home with no atonement needed, regardless of the imminent awakening that's about to challenge the Earth.

Chung also stated that if all the world's inhabitants had been able to break free from their loops, then the great awakening would not need to occur, thus highlighting the importance of reliving and re-evaluating past experiences in our loops. Furthermore, the forthcoming awakening is clearly essential to help many people achieve this feat.

Chung stated that the prize at the end of this conflict is worth every battle, which suggests that at the end of the day, light will always succeed darkness in every walk of life, and that everlasting love will always prevail.

ISAC said that no more words are needed as we now approach our great awakening. It is now up to the people of the Earth to heed these words and rise to the challenge that faces society.

ISAC reiterated Chung's thoughts on materialism and how the effects of greed may tempt souls to drift from their path in order to seek out a perfect establishment.

Chung stated that when we finally break free from our loops and return home then it will be to a place of ultimate riches with absolutely no regrets.

ISAC confirmed that the greatest challenge to mankind is not death, but in fact life. We should not fear the thought of dying when this great awakening commences, but rather the thought of not living through it with all that we have learned from this experiment.

Finally, Gordon came forward and gave us all personal messages of hope for our future.

He informed me that Kane and Abel will soon face each other in a mighty battle. Both enemies will put forward an enticing case for the people of our world to join their side and rid this world of whatever they believe is affecting its survival.

I asked Gordon which side the people should choose and he replied that they should only choose to concentrate on breaking free from their personal loop. Only when that feat has been accomplished will the people of this world be able to summon the strength of mind to refuse to join either side. On that day, the slumbering dragon will be fully awake, and we will have reached the end of our beginning. Gordon's message to me was simply to remind people of this statement whenever they began to slumber.

On reflection, I felt that the most intriguing statement of this whole book came from ISAC's summarisation - 'there will come a time when physical bodies cannot die and all emotions will be eradicated.'

But that's another story!

ACKNOWLEDGEMENTS

First of all, I think it's only appropriate that I thank my spirit team and all the other spirit people for everything they have given us over the last six years. When I think back to the first evening that we sat for trance I never thought it would last for more than a few weeks, never mind over six years. If only I knew then that it was always much more than just inviting mediums to develop their skills to a higher level. The importance of this experiment really only hit home when we began to realise the extent of the forthcoming worldwide events.

On a personal level, without this experiment I may not have been able to identify and break free from my own loop. This was achieved in 2021 after completing my previous book '2020 The End of the Beginning' which was the precursor for all that was brought forward in this publication. Without my spirit team in tow, this would have been an extremely arduous task to accomplish and the events about to unfold would have been far more challenging in every aspect.

Of course, it wasn't just me personally that benefitted from the work of the spirit guides. Every single person involved in this experiment had the pleasure to work alongside these incredibly gifted and insightful souls. This even stretched to the caretaker of the community hall where the Stars from Above Sanctuary was held every month. He never knew (maybe just as well) that every month he was subconsciously told how many chairs to set out for the monthly meeting. And he was never wrong! In fact, on one occasion to my surprise there seemed to be an extra seat left out for us. However, one of the sitters who had contacted me earlier to say that they couldn't make it, unexpectedly managed to arrive on time. It's not often that my spirit team surprise me, but they did on this occasion. It's worth noting that I also run a monthly mediumship training group and suffice to say I have to adjust the number of chairs left out by the caretaker in this particular group. This shows the significant difference in working with higher level guides.

It's fair to say that spirit guides of this calibre do possess the ability to influence people from all walks of life; although they will only do this if the need arises. In this case, for the purposes of completing this experiment.

Indebted thanks must go to the five trance mediums that were used in this publication. I do know that for the last twelve months in particular it has been a struggle for them to contain everything that has been digested as part of these sessions, and also when they have been meditating at home. This has been a full-time job and not just a few hours per month.

In my opinion, the level of trance mediumship with these five mediums was phenomenal, and I do hope that they all continue this vocation in whatever path they now find themselves on.

The sitters in the group also did an amazing job. Their dedication to this project was second to none and I can only thank them from the bottom of my heart. They were all accomplished trance mediums who had trained over the last few years, and even though they weren't used for trance in the final year, they were all vitally important in ensuring that the blend of energies was just perfect for everything to take place.

Special thanks have to go to the three ladies who organised the monthly sessions. These special people gave up more than just their time for this project. As well as being sitters in the project, they also continue to run a weekly spiritualist church. In fact, two mediums who attended this church eventually joined our trance group and became two of the trance medium used in this experiment. This may not have happened but for the sterling work done by Anne Hagon, Helen McMaster, and Margaret Davidson.

Deep trance mediumship is not for everyone. Many experienced mediums joined our group but found that their expertise lay elsewhere. It takes many dedicated years of practice to become an accomplished trance medium and I have to thank my own mentors and teachers for encouraging me to chase this dream. I only hope that I have passed this message on to the people involved in this experiment.

One of the ways that I would train the group to strengthen their level of deep meditation required to invoke deep trance channelling, was to sit in a circle and stretch out their left arm to sit neatly on top of the shoulder of the person sitting to their left. I would encourage them to keep their arm sitting there until the meditation would end. I would like to invite you to try this at home and see how long you can keep your arm outstretched whilst gently resting on a support. The average time would be around two to three minutes before your arm becomes stiff and sore. Our group could keep their arms in place for over thirty minutes, and some of the group were over seventy years old. It is incredible how you can achieve certain things if your mind can become so focussed that your physical body becomes almost redundant to pain.

I would finally like to thank you personally for reading these words. I hope that this book helps in whatever predicament that you may find yourself in. As previously stated – our test of character, resolve, and resilience will almost certainly be stretched to the extreme in the coming months and years. This will undoubtedly be the greatest challenge in your physical lifetime, but also the most perfect time to finally address the constraints within your energy loop.

Only you can decide on your next step forward in life… just as it has always been.

Other books by the author:

'An Average Joe's Search for the Meaning of Life'
'Ghost Writers'
'New Mediumship' (spiritcounsellor)
'2020 The End of the Beginning'

All available on amazon kindle and
most other online bookstores.

Printed in Great Britain
by Amazon

51021339R00106